Literacy Play
Over 300 Dramatic Play Ac
That Teach Pre-Reading S

Also Available from Sherrie West and Amy Cox

SAND & WATER PLAY
Simple, Creative Activities for Young Children

Literacy Play • Over 300 Dramatic Play Activities That Teach Pre-Reading Skills

Literacy Play

Over 300 Dramatic Play Activities That Teach Pre-Reading Skills

**Sherrie West
& Amy Cox
Illustrated by Kathy
Dobbs**

gryphon house, Inc.
Beltsville, MD

Copyright

Illustrations: Kathy Dobbs
Cover Art: Straight Shots®, Ellicott City, Maryland

Library of Congress Cataloging-in-Publication Information

West, Sherrie, 1957-
  Literacy play : over 300 dramatic play activities that teach pre-reading skills / by Sherrie West and Amy Cox.
     p. cm.
  ISBN 0-87659-292-2
  1. Language arts (Early childhood) 2. Play. 3. Early childhood education--Activity programs. 4. Drama in education. I. Cox, Amy, 1968- II. Title.
  LB1139.5.L35W37 2004
  372.6--dc22

                                                    2003020454

Bulk Purchase

Gryphon House books are available for special premiums and sales promotions as well as for fund-raising use. Special editions or book excerpts also can be created to specification. For details, contact the Director of Marketing at Gryphon House.

Disclaimer

Gryphon House, Inc. and the authors cannot be held responsible for damage, mishap, or injury incurred during the use of or because of activities in this book. Appropriate and reasonable caution and adult supervision of children involved in activities and corresponding to the age and capability of each child involved, is recommended at all times. Do not leave children unattended at any time. Observe safety and caution at all times.

Table of Contents

Table of Contents

CHAPTER 8—READING, WRITING, AND TALKING 163

Introduction

We wrote this book to help teachers understand that literacy skills can be taught through play. Children learn best through hands-on experiences that are meaningful to them. Often, parents and teachers feel that children are only learning when they are doing worksheets or practicing their alphabet. Emergent literacy is more than drill and practice—it is not just teaching children the letters of the alphabet. Literacy is a developmental process, it is understanding concepts and applying them to the world. When children are engaged in group activities that expose them to both oral and written language, they learn to read and write naturally. Concepts become real, rather than arbitrary. Because the ideas and concepts are familiar to them they are no longer abstract. Dramatic play can be a place where children engage in, practice, and apply literacy concepts. By putting children in an enriched literacy environment, they can practice, experiment, and explore oral and written language. Dramatic play and literacy go hand in hand with activities that address the needs, skills, and interests of the children in your classroom.

The activities in this book are designed to give children opportunities to discover literacy concepts in a natural environment or setting. As children engage in dramatic play, they use print in a meaningful way. Children see adults making lists, writing checks, reading the newspaper, following instructions, and writing notes. Teachers can use this medium to teach children literacy in their classrooms by surrounding children with environmental print, books, signs, messages, lists, notes, and so on. In dramatic play children interact with these kinds of props. They also use oral language to communicate their needs and ideas to peers. As a teacher, you can create an environment that supports literacy through dramatic play.

There are several different components of literacy: oral language, written language, understanding print, phonological awareness, reading comprehension, and book appreciation. These components are used interactively and support each other. They do not always follow a sequential order. All of these components develop simultaneously and work together to create emergent readers and writers.

Oral Language Continuum (the first four listed occur from one to three years of age)

- making sounds ("Da, Da;" "Ma, Ma;" "Wa, Wa")
- saying simple meaningful words ("Mama," "Dada," "no," "more")
- using two-word sentences ("me drink," "me want")
- using three-word sentences ("me want more")
- using short complete sentences ("I want a drink")
- stopping to listen
- sharing information
- taking turns talking
- carrying on a purposeful conversation
- writing oral language

Writing Continuum

- circular scribbles
- horizontal scribbles
- separate scribble marks
- separate marks with beginning forms
- letter-like forms and letters
- letters

2003 Heads Up! Reading, National Head Start Association

Print Awareness Continuum

- print is different than pictures
- print conveys meaning
- print has practical uses
- letter knowledge
- words are separated by spaces
- words are made up of letters
- capitalization
- punctuation

adapted from 2003 Heads Up! Reading, National Head Start Association

Phonological Awareness Continuum

Discriminative listening is the foundation that moves children into Phonological Awareness Continuum.

- rhyming
- alliteration
- sentence segmentation
- syllable blending and segmenting
- onset-rhyme blending and segmenting
- phoneme blending, segmenting and manipulation

Texas Center for Reading and Language Arts

Reading Comprehension

▶ attending to pictures
▶ learning new words and meanings
▶ sequencing events
▶ questions and answers
▶ retelling stories

Book Appreciation

▶ book handling skills
▶ sharing of books with others
▶ love of reading and books
▶ motivation to read because of love of books

How to Use This Book

This book is divided into eight chapters: occupations, home, nature, science, stores, transportation, performers, and literary. Within each chapter, there are a variety of sections that focus on different dramatic play areas. Each dramatic play area has the following components: literacy application, literacy objectives, spotlight words, materials, props, setting up, open-ended questions, making books, extension activities, and literacy resources, which includes songs, poems, and fingerplays, and a book list.

Literacy Application

This section is designed to help teachers understand how to teach different literacy concepts more effectively and assess where children are on the literacy continua. It explains the importance of teaching literacy in appropriate ways.

Literacy Objectives

Objectives can be long-term or short-term goals. Short-term goals, which are generated from long-term goals, give direction to daily teaching. They should be specific to the individuals in your class. The objectives for each activity in this book are goals we believe can be met through that specific activity. When doing an activity, you can focus on one, two, or more of the suggested objectives. However, if none of the suggested objectives are appropriate for you, change them to fit the needs of the children in your care.

As you incorporate the objectives into your lesson plans, make sure they are measurable and can be met. The only way a teacher knows whether an objective has been met or a child has learned something is through evaluating and comparing what the child already knew with what the child now knows. The teacher knows if the activity is effective if she or he can see a changed outcome in the child's behavior through observation. Evaluation is critical. If the desired objective is not met and does not enhance the child's development, reassess the child's needs and make new short-term goals.

If you do not meet your long-term goals, then develop different short-term goals or consider the possibility that what you want the children to learn is not appropriate for their developmental sequence. Activities should reflect the needs, skills, and interests of the children in your classroom.

Spotlight Words

These are vocabulary words that relate to the dramatic play focus. Use these words in your verbal communication with the children to help them understand their meaning. You can also write these words on chart paper to expose children to written print on a daily basis.

Materials

Start out simply. As you view the list of materials needed in each activity, identify a few props that you will collect, remembering that it can take several years to gather all the materials listed. Ask businesses and parents to donate materials to help cut the cost of your supplies. If you approach businesses and organizations, many will donate money or supplies, such as books, paper, and other materials. Hunt for bargains in dollar stores. Use your resources to find materials to enhance the literacy environment in your classroom.

Props

Often, children need a prop to help stimulate ideas to bring into their play. The suggested props add unique literacy experiences that encourage children's creativity. They are a supplement to the materials, enriching the environment and capturing the children's interest as they read and write. It exposes them to print from real-life situations, for example, order pads for the restaurant, library cards for the library, sign-in sheets for the doctor's office, checks for the grocery store, or invitations for a birthday party. Props should never be used as worksheets. Worksheets stifle creativity. Involve the children as much as possible in making the props prior to setting up the dramatic play activity, so that the children can use them during their play.

Setting Up

Dramatic play evolves naturally when you set up props that promote play with a specific focus, such as a grocery store, a camping trip, or a library. Make sure that each of the dramatic play areas are arranged appropriately. For example, when you set up the doctor's office, make sure you rearrange the furniture and equipment to look like a doctor's office with a waiting room. Provide specific instructions if they are necessary. At other times, provide broad, simple guidelines for setting up the activity.

Open-Ended Questions

Asking children open-ended questions during their dramatic play experience will help them think and discover on their own. Find a balance between asking too few questions and too many questions that might dominate or take over children's play. Because questioning is an important way a teacher can stimulate learning, we have included an extended list of open-ended questions or statements below.

How might you group them?
How could you change what happened?
How could you figure out...?
How could you organize _____ to show_____?
How did that happen?
How does this work?
How is...?
How is it related to...?
How would you describe...?
How would you explain...?
How would you solve _____ with what you have learned?
Suppose you could _____, what would you do?
What can you say about_____?
What choices could you make?
What do you suppose we learned?
What evidence can you find?
What is...?
What is your main idea?
What other way would you do it?
What would happen if...?
What would you do differently?
When did _____ happen?
When did...?
Where is...?
Why did...?

Why did you choose that?
Why do you think...?
Would it be better if...?

Making Books

Making books is an extension activity. Children can make these books, which will reinforce the knowledge they gained during their play experience.

There are reproducible pages (see Appendix) to make books for some of the dramatic play areas; others are described in detail to get you started. These child-created books are class and individual books. In a class book, each child adds his or her own page to create one book. A class book usually stays in the classroom for an extended period of time. An individual book is created by one child and is usually taken home.

It is important that children have the opportunity to create books. When children make class books or individual books, they become readers and writers. They apply the literacy concepts they have learned while making their own books. They learn to associate oral language with written language, to sequence events, to compose their own stories, and write at their own levels. Children may write using meaningful scribbling, using letter-like forms, making a series of letters, asking for the spelling, or sounding out the words themselves. As children write books, they are motivated to develop their skills at increasingly higher levels. When teachers provide children with opportunities to make books, they are also helping children to gain confidence and believe they are readers and writers. Because of the excitement and enthusiasm children have when making their own books, they have a strong desire to keep and re-read their own books. Allowing children to make their own books is a special and meaningful activity for children and teachers.

Extension Activities

These activities enhance children's understanding, and they can be done before or after the original activity.

Literacy Resources

Songs, poems, and fingerplays teach children many important pre-reading skills. They help children build vocabulary, develop memory capacity, hear syllables, gain phonological awareness, learn auditory discrimination, play with rhyming, understand sequencing, and hear the rhythm and flow of language. As children learn fingerplays, songs, and poems, they develop a love of words and language.

Introduce children to songs, poems, and fingerplays before, during, or after dramatic play activities. For example, teach children songs, poems, and fingerplays as part of circle or group time, write them on chart paper and hang them in the dramatic play area, or sing them as a follow-up activity.

The book list is a great tool to support dramatic play. Books help children reenact stories or give factual information about their play, and give them a basic knowledge to act out realistic or imaginary roles. Reading is one of the best things you can do to help children become real readers. We have provided a list of quality picture books appropriate for children ages three through six.

Occupations

Doctor's Office

LITERACY APPLICATION

Circular and Horizontal Scribbling

Scribbling is the first step in the process of learning to write. Encourage children to experiment at all levels of writing. Children mimic writing by drawing lines, rows of circles, or letters. Preschoolers can distinguish between drawing pictures and writing. When children scribble on prescription pads, clipboards, and sign-in sheets in the doctor's office, they are writing.

LITERACY OBJECTIVES

Children will:

▶ recognize and read their own names and their classmates' names on sign-in sheets.

▶ pretend to read environmental print such as magazines.

▶ attempt to write using alphabet letters when writing prescriptions and writing diagnoses on clipboards.

SPOTLIGHT WORDS

arms • brain • ears • eyes • germs • head • heart • legs • lungs • prescriptions • reflexes • skeleton • x-rays

Literacy Play • Over 300 Dramatic Play Activities That Teach Pre-Reading Skills

MATERIALS

arm sling • bandages • Band-Aids • bathroom scale • booties • clipboards •
cots • cotton balls • empty pill bottles • magazines • nurse's hats • pencils •
play syringes • rubber gloves • stethoscopes • surgical masks • white coats
(or large white shirts with the sleeves cut to size) • x-rays

PROPS

▶ **Prescription Pad**: Staple together small squares of paper, with a
space for the child's name and the doctor's name at
the top of each square.

▶ **Sign-in Sheet**: Write the name of the doctor at the
top, make a column on the left for the patient's name,
and a column on the right for the time the patient
arrives.

▶ **Eye Chart** (see page 184 in Appendix): Make a copy of this
page and hang it in the doctor's office.

SETTING UP

Set up the dramatic play area to
look like a waiting room and
doctor's office. You could also use
the block area to be a hospital and
the sand and water table to be a
pharmacy. Create an area in the
waiting room for the children to sign
in. Put paper, pencils, and a telephone at
the reception desk. Place magazines and
books in the waiting room for the
patients to read. Set up the doctor's
office with medical equipment and dress-
up props. Make sure there are clipboards
for the doctors to write notes on and
order prescriptions. To support the
activities, find age-appropriate books at your
local library for the children to explore.

OPEN-ENDED QUESTIONS

What does a doctor do?

How do you know when you are sick?

Why do we get sick?

Why do we need to sleep every night?

Why do we need to eat three meals a day?

How do you exercise?

What happens when you use your hands to cover your mouth when you cough?

MAKING BOOKS

▶ **All About My Body** (individual book): Write the following sentences on separate pieces of paper (or you can write two sentences per page). Staple the pages together and on the title page, write "All About My Body" by: _____.

> *I have two arms and two hands.*
> *This is my heart.*
> *This is my brain.*
> *These are my lungs.*
> *These are my intestines.*
> *These are my bones.*
> *These are my muscles.*
> *I have two legs and two feet.*
> *This is my body!*

Encourage the children to illustrate their books with their own pictures. Ask the children what the different body parts can do and add it to the corresponding text.

▶ **"Dem" Bones** (individual or class book): Encourage the children to draw pictures of their bodies, including their bones (skeleton). Encourage them to label their body parts using scribble marks. Ask each child about what he has written and illustrated.

EXTENSION ACTIVITIES

1) Take a field trip to a doctor's office or hospital, or invite a nurse or doctor to visit your classroom to tell the children about his or her career.

2) During circle time, encourage the children to role play what a doctor would do if he or she was sick. Write down their responses on a chart and post it in the doctor's office dramatic play area to stimulate discussion during play.

3) Teach the children how to wash their hands properly. Also discuss germs and how they can make people sick.

4) Take a petri dish and ask the children to touch one side with their fingers. Keep the other side untouched. Put out both sides and let the children watch the germs grow.

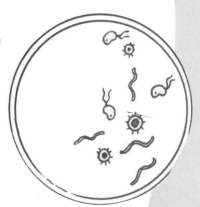

LITERACY RESOURCES— SONGS, POEMS, AND FINGERPLAYS

Miss Polly (traditional)
Miss Polly had a dolly
Who was sick, sick, sick. (cradle doll in arms)
So she called for the doctor
To come quick, quick, quick. (pretend to use telephone)

The doctor came with his bag and his hat (hand on head)
And he knocked on the door
With a rat-a-tat-tat. (knock on floor)

He looked at the dolly
And he shook his head
And he said, "Miss Polly,
Put her straight to bed." (shake finger)

"I'll write a prescription (write on hand)
For a pill, pill, pill.
I'll be back in the morning
With my bill, bill, bill." (put hand out with bill)

Tissues (West and Cox)
A runny nose,
A little sneeze,
Grab a tissue,
Will you please?

LITERACY RESOURCES—BOOK LIST

Busy Toes by C.W. Bowie
Doctors by Dee Ready
I Have a Weird Brother Who Digested a Fly by Joan Holub
There Was an Old Lady Who Swallowed a Fly by Simms Taback

Detective

LITERACY APPLICATION

Questions and Answers

When children are asked questions and encouraged to give oral answers, their vocabulary increases and they gain an understanding of the meanings of words. Children need opportunities to freely share information in conversations with each other. When they pretend to be detectives, they will need to ask questions ("What is it?" or "Where can it be?"). As they become more involved in questioning, their understanding of language will increase. Assess how well a child understands oral language by listening to his or her questions and conversations.

LITERACY OBJECTIVES

Children will:
▶ use one object to represent another.
▶ explain the meaning of their own drawings.
▶ tell stories using pictures.
▶ pretend to read by attending to clues when looking at pictures with labels.
▶ enjoy language by being exposed to riddles.

SPOTLIGHT WORDS

clues • detective • fingerprints • listen • look • observe

MATERIALS

clipboards • clues • coats • hats • magnifying glasses • pencils

PROPS

◗ **Report Form**: Write "Investigation Report" at the top of the paper. Then fill in the rest of the paper with the following details, leaving a space after each line:

  Detective:

  Location:

  Time of Day:

  Number of Suspects:

  Description:

◗ **Detective Badge** (see page 185 in Appendix): Make copies of the detective badge and let the children write their names on them.

◗ **Fingerprint Card** (see page 186 in Appendix): Make copies of the fingerprint card for the children to put their prints on.

SETTING UP

Put out detective props and encourage the children to be detectives. Attach the report form prop (see above) to a clipboard and ask the children to record their findings. Choose one of the following activities to set up with the dramatic play materials to enhance their play.

1) Put the children into groups (with a teacher) and let them record sounds in their environment using tape recorders. When the children come back, let them take turns guessing and describing what the sounds are. Encourage conversations between the children.

2) Have a mystery hunt. Hide clues (pictures with written labels) on the playground or inside the school. Have three different sets of color-coordinated clues. Divide the children into three groups, and assign each group one of the three colors. Let the children find the clues that lead them to the solution. For example: "What happened to the lost pencil sharpener?" Clues: Look for the pipes that bring water into our classroom; Go to the place that is green and growing; Go to the place where you hang up your coat; and so on.

3) Hide die-cut letters on the playground or in your classroom. Write each letter of the alphabet on separate paper bags. Encourage the children to find the letters and match them to the appropriate bag.

OPEN-ENDED QUESTIONS

What happened first?
What happened next?
What came last?

MAKING BOOKS

▶ **I Spy With My Little Eye** (individual or class book): Give the children magnifying glasses and encourage them to find things. Ask them questions about what they found and listen to their answers. Encourage the children to draw the things they saw in their own books or on pieces of paper (to be compiled into a class book). Children can then dictate what they saw or write it themselves with help.

EXTENSION ACTIVITIES

1) Play a memory game. Place several items on a tray. Ask the children to look closely at the objects. Then cover them with a towel and remove one of the items. Uncover the tray and see if the children can remember which item is missing. Give them clues if they don't know.

2) Make several questions or riddles and write them on strips of paper. Pull them out of a hat and let the children give the answers. For example: What is gray, has a long nose, and has big ears?

3) Play "I Spy." Let the children take turns giving clues that describe an object in the room and the other children guess what it is. For example: "I see something that is red, round, and tastes good. What is it?"

4) Make secret messages using lemon juice or milk. Dip a toothpick into lemon juice or milk, and write a message. Let it dry, put it under a light bulb, and your invisible message will appear.

LITERACY RESOURCES— SONGS, POEMS, AND FINGERPLAYS

What Am I? (West and Cox)

I am a star,
That lives in the sea.
I have legs and arms,
but no fins on me.
What am I?
(Answer: a starfish)

I Spy With My Little Eye (West and Cox)

I spy with my little eye
Something flying by.
It has four wings, it's not a fly
It flutters in the sky.
What am I?
(Answer: a dragonfly)

I spy with my little eye
Treats for birds and I,
They grow in the tree, they're red, that's why,
You'll find them in a pie.
What am I?
(Answer: cherries)

I spy with my little eye
Something low not high,
Some shoes have it, "Oh me, Oh my,"
It's knotted like a tie.
What am I?
(Answer: a shoelace)

I spy with my little eye
A trunk you don't see in a car,
It's too big for a house,
But it's scared of a mouse.
What am I?
(Answer: an elephant's trunk)

LITERACY RESOURCES—BOOK LIST

The Amazing I Spy ABC by Ken Laidlaw
I Spy Mystery: A Book of Picture Riddles by Jean Marzollo
It Looked Like Spilt Milk by Charles G. Shaw
Look Book by Tana Hoban
Officer Buckle and Gloria by Peggy Rathmann

Veterinarian

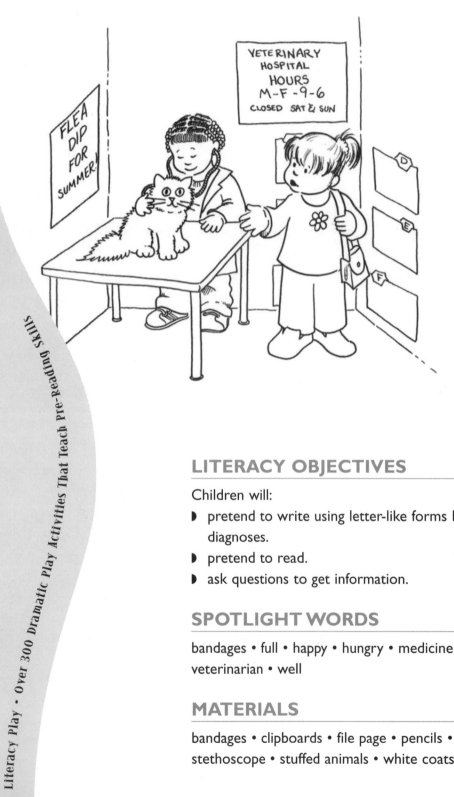

FLEA DIP FOR SUMMER

VETERINARY HOSPITAL HOURS M-F-9-6 CLOSED SAT & SUN

LITERACY APPLICATION

Stopping to Listen

When children learn to stop and listen, they are achieving one of the steps of taking turns in conversations. Listening is focusing attention on one thing at a time. As the children's listening skills develop, they attend to each other and communication is enhanced. For example, when a child plays the role of veterinarian, he or she must stop to listen to the needs of the pet's owner. Then the owner of the pet must stop and listen to the vet's diagnosis.

LITERACY OBJECTIVES

Children will:

▶ pretend to write using letter-like forms by writing their pet's names and diagnoses.
▶ pretend to read.
▶ ask questions to get information.

SPOTLIGHT WORDS

bandages • full • happy • hungry • medicine • sad • shots • sick • veterinarian • well

MATERIALS

bandages • clipboards • file page • pencils • play syringes • signs • stethoscope • stuffed animals • white coats

PROPS

▶ **Pet Nametag**: Draw a few nametag shapes on paper, such as a bone shape, a circle, and so on. Make a few copies and cut them out. The children can write their pet's names on them and attach them to stuffed animals.

▶ **Pet Care**: Cut paper in half. Write "My Pet" at the top of each half. Then fill in the rest of the paper with the following details, leaving a space after each line:

Name of Pet:
Kind of Pet:
Special Care:

SETTING UP

Set up your dramatic play area to look like a veterinarian's office. Help the children make "Open," "Closed," and other signs for the office. Let the children use the clipboards to make notes. Have slips of paper for the children to write their pets' names on. Write the letters of the alphabet on file folders and encourage the children to file pictures of different animals according to their first letter.

OPEN-ENDED QUESTIONS

How does an animal cry?
What did you do to help it stop crying?
What and how do animals eat?
Why do you feed your pets certain things?
How can you tell if your pet is sick or well? Happy or sad?
How can you make your pet feel better?

MAKING BOOKS

▶ **If I Had a…** (individual or class book): Ask the children how they would take care of different animals. Give the children pages with the sentence "If I had a _____, I would…" at the top. Ask them to fill in the blank with the name of an animal and how to care for it. For example: "If I had an elephant, I would feed him peanuts." Encourage the children to illustrate their own page or book. When the children are telling you about their books, make a conscious effort to stop and listen.

EXTENSION ACTIVITIES

1) Invite a vet to visit your classroom or go on a field trip to an animal hospital and teach the children how to take care of different animals.

2) Ask the children to classify different animals.

LITERACY RESOURCES—
SONGS, POEMS, AND FINGERPLAYS

Bingo (traditional)

There was a farmer had a dog
And Bingo was his name-o.
B-I-N-G-O
B-I-N-G-O
B-I-N-G-O
And Bingo was his name-o.

(Repeat, clapping one more letter for each additional verse until you are only clapping.)

clap-I-N-G-O
clap-clap-N-G-O...

The Turtle (traditional)

The turtle crawls on the ground
And makes a rustling sound.
He carries his house
Wherever he goes,
And when he is scared,
He pulls in his nose and covers his toes!

LITERACY RESOURCES—BOOK LIST

Let's Talk About Tongues by Allan Fowler
Veterinarians by Dee Ready

Dentist

LITERACY APPLICATION

Alliteration: First Sound of One's Name

Introduce children to the sounds of letters by drawing attention to the first letter sound in their own names. It is natural for a child to say, "That's my name" when he sees the first letter of his name in another word. Point out other children whose names begin with the same letter as his. Children can practice hearing the first sound of their names when filing their patient charts in the dentist's office. Encourage the children to brainstorm by coming up with words that begin with the same letter as their first names, such as Bob, ball, bat, bee, book, baby, and so on. Children will be more interested in words that are meaningful to them.

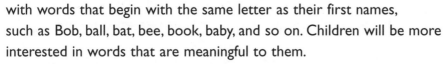

LITERACY OBJECTIVES

Children will:
▶ recognize and read their own names and the names of their classmates as they use the patient files in the play area.
▶ be exposed to the sounds of letters as they file names on dental forms.
▶ practice writing using letter-like forms.
▶ pretend to read brochures.

SPOTLIGHT WORDS

bacteria • brush • cavities • certificate • files • floss • fluoride • gums • hygienist • teeth • toothbrush • toothpaste

MATERIALS

big plastic teeth • dental bibs • dental pamphlets • file folders • fun stickers • gloves • mask • report forms • small cups • teeth literature • teeth posters • toothbrushes • trays • white coats

PROPS

▶ **Dental Chart File:** Write "Dental Chart" at the top of each child's paper. Underneath, write the following items, leaving a space after each one:

Patient's Name:
Date:
Findings:

▶ **Dental Certificates:** Make certificates by drawing a border around a piece of paper. Turn the paper sideways so it is horizontal. Write the following information, centering it to look like a certificate:

Congratulations!
You have no cavities! Dr. _____ is proud that you are keeping your teeth clean. Proudly presented to _____ on _____.

Make a few copies and encourage the children to decorate them with dental-related illustrations (such as a toothbrush, tooth, or smile).

SETTING UP

Set up the dramatic play area to look like a dental office with a waiting and examining room. Place name cards nearby for the children. Ask the children to write their names on file folders (dental files) using the name cards. Then encourage the children to file their dental forms under the correct letter. Help the children hear the first sound of their names. The children can hand out fun stickers and dental certificates to patients.

OPEN-ENDED QUESTIONS

Why do we need to brush our teeth?
Why do we use toothpaste?
How do your teeth grow?
How many teeth do you need?

MAKING BOOKS

▶ **My Tooth** (individual book): Make a copy of the tooth pattern (see page 204 in the Appendix). Staple this page to about four sheets of plain paper and cut out the tooth shape from all the pages. This saves time and ensures that the poem is on the first page of the book only. Give a book to each child and encourage the children to make up a story. They can illustrate and write the words with help or dictate their stories for an adult to write. While helping the child write his story, emphasize each word that starts with the same sound as the child's name. For example, if the child's name is Timmy, as you write "tooth" or "took," emphasize the "T" sound.

▶ **Lost Tooth Record** (class book): Cut out tooth shapes using the tooth pattern from the previous activity. Cut and staple enough pages so that each child has one. Record when each child lost his tooth. Take photos of the children, and let them glue their photo to their tooth page. Ask the children to write their names and the date on their pages. This is a good book to keep in the classroom all year.

Note: If the children in your class have not yet lost any teeth, change the title to "First Tooth Record." Ask the children to find out when they got their first tooth and write that date on the page.

EXTENSION ACTIVITIES

1) Invite a dental hygienist to come to your classroom and teach the children about how to keep their teeth healthy.

2) Let the children brush their teeth and then chew a plaque dye tablet (available at a dentist's office or pharmacy) to see where they need to brush better.

3) Put toothbrushes, toothpaste, and empty 1-liter soda bottles (with the tops cut off) in the sand and water table. Let the children practice brushing on the soda bottles.

LITERACY RESOURCES— SONGS, POEMS, AND FINGERPLAYS

I Wiggle My Tooth (West and Cox)

I wiggle my tooth,
With all my might.
Hoping the tooth fairy,
Will come tonight.

She will take my tooth,
While I'm asleep.
A penny, a nickel,
Or dime I'll keep.

I Brush My Teeth (West and Cox)

I brush my teeth,
To keep them bright.
To make them strong,
Clean and white.

I brush my teeth,
Morning, noon and night.
Soft little circles,
All around, just right.

LITERACY RESOURCES—BOOK LIST

Just Going to the Dentist by Mercer Mayer
The Selfish Crocodile by Faustin Charles

Firefighter

LITERACY APPLICATION

Learning New Words and Meanings: Prepositions

It is important for children to learn the meanings of prepositions such as *in, out, over, under,* and *behind.* When children gain an understanding of prepositional words, it increases their skills in becoming beginning readers. As children play as firefighters, they are going in and out of a "burning" structure, and over and under the structure. This provides the opportunity to teach children the meaning of these words in a hands-on way.

LITERACY OBJECTIVES

Children will:

▶ practice writing their names using alphabet letters on their badges.

▶ understand the meaning of print when they see it on labels and maps.

SPOTLIGHT WORDS

behind • boots • coat • down • fire engine • fire escape • fire hat • fire hose • in • mask • out • over • oxygen tank • smoke • under • up

MATERIALS

boots • fire hats • flashlights • jackets • labels • large blocks or snap walls • maps • old vacuum hoses for fire hoses • steering wheel • step stool ladder

PROPS

- **Firefighter Badges** (see page 185 in the Appendix): Make copies of the badge and let the children write their names on them.
- **Stop, Drop, and Roll Certificate**: Make certificates by cutting paper in half and writing the following information:

    This is to certify that _____ *can stop, drop, and roll.*

    _____ *(date).* Illustrate as desired.

SETTING UP

Turn your dramatic play area into a fire station. Label the different areas and equipment with cards. Set out the firefighter props and ask the children to write their names on their badges. Encourage the children to create a structure from large blocks or use a climber to make a house. The children (firefighters) will put out an imaginary fire on the structure. Also, encourage the children to make a fire engine using a steering wheel, blocks, and so on. As the children play, point out where they are by using preposition words such as: *under* the structure, *in* the fire engine, spray *on top of* the fire, *around* a house, and *behind* the house. You can also make labels of prepositions to put on the structure, fire station, and fire engine.

OPEN-ENDED QUESTIONS

Why do firefighters wear uniforms?
What can you do to be safe if there is a fire?
What should you do if you find some matches?

MAKING BOOKS

- **Fire, Fire** (individual book): Make a copy of the house pattern (see page 202 in the Appendix) and firefighter (page 201) and seven copies of the door pattern (page 201). Write the following words on the doors (one word per door): "Above," "Behind," "In," "Out," "Under," "Beside," and "Around." Make enough copies so that each child gets one house, one firefighter, and seven doors. Cut out the door pages and staple them on top of the door on the house pattern. Attach a curly ribbon to the firefighter's hose, and attach the hose to the bottom corner of the house. Ask the children to draw pictures of the firefighter on the door pages following the preposition words. Children can move the firefighter according to the preposition words relating to the house. For example, *under* the house, *over* the house, and so on.

EXTENSION ACTIVITIES

1) Talk about fire safety. Teach the children how to stop, drop, and roll; leave matches alone; and call 911 in an emergency.
2) Invite a firefighter to come and visit your classroom.

LITERACY RESOURCES—
SONGS, POEMS, AND FINGERPLAYS

Ten Little Firefighters (traditional)
Ten little firefighters, sleeping in a row (line up fingers)
Ding, ding goes the bell
And down the pole they go. (pretend to go down the pole)
Off on the engine oh, oh, oh (make the siren noise)
Using the big hose, so, so, so. (pretend to hold the hose)
When all the fire's out,
Home so slow
Back into bed, all in a row. (stretch out fingers and curl them into the palm of your hands)

Firefighters Out of Bed (West and Cox)

Out of bed,
Firefighters jump.
Quickly get ready,
Without a bump.

Through a hole,
And down a pole.
In the fire truck.
Now let's go.

Grab your boots,
Put them on.
Bell is ringing,
Ding, ding, dong.

Big, red trucks,
Race to the fire.
Hoses spraying,
Flames expire.

LITERACY RESOURCES—BOOK LIST

Fire! Fire! by Gail Gibbons
Emergency! by Gail Gibbons
Fire Fighters by Norma Simon
Fire Fighter! by Angela Royston

Banker

LITERACY APPLICATION

Complete Sentences

Children communicate orally to others as they play. Support children's language development by giving them opportunities to talk and encouraging them to move to the next level on the oral language continuum, which is stopping to listen and sharing information with others. When children pretend to go to the bank, they interact with customers and employees. They ask for money and respond appropriately to questions.

LITERACY OBJECTIVES

Children will:

▶ talk to others as they interact at the bank.

▶ practice using letter-like forms by writing on checks and deposit slips.

▶ understand the meaning of print by seeing print on money, checks, deposit slips, and so on.

SPOTLIGHT WORDS

banker • change • coins • deposit • earn • less • loans • more • save • teller • withdraw

MATERIALS

boxes for money • calculators • large blocks • number strip • old credit cards • paper • pencils • planners • purses • wallets

PROPS

▶ **Deposit Slips** (see page 187 in the Appendix).
▶ **Paychecks** (see page 187 in the Appendix).
▶ **Credit Cards** (see page 196 in the Appendix).
▶ **Checks** (see page 196 in the Appendix).
▶ **Play Money**: Use Monopoly money, or make your own.

SETTING UP

Encourage the children to create a drive-through for their bank using large blocks. Show them how to make a counter out of blocks for the bank teller to stand behind and a box to slip the money out to the customer. Put out the banker props and materials. The bank customers use checks, deposit slips, and so on to write on. The bank teller can count the money using a number strip, if needed.

OPEN-ENDED QUESTIONS

If you had a handful of pennies, what would you buy?
Why is it important to save money?

MAKING BOOKS

▶ **If I Were a Millionaire** (class book): Brainstorm with the children about things they would do if they had a lot of money. The children will probably mention a lot of things they could buy, but also encourage them to think of the things they could do with the money to help others. For example, "If I were a millionaire, I would give money to _____ to help _____." This is a good opportunity to teach some values. Encourage the children to use complete sentences to express their ideas. Ask the children to draw and write what they would do with the money, and then staple all the pages together to make a book. On the title page, write, "If I Were a Millionaire…" Read the book at circle time.

EXTENSION ACTIVITIES

1) Let the children make their own play money. Put out real bills and coins for the children to look at while they are drawing.
2) Teach the children about the different values of money.
3) Set up a token (money) system in your classroom. Let the children earn tokens by doing certain jobs or requirements. Then let them use their tokens to buy privileges or rewards.

LITERACY RESOURCES— SONGS, POEMS, AND FINGERPLAYS

Five Quarters (West and Cox)
Five little quarters, I used them at the store,
I bought an ice cream scoop; then there were four.

Four little quarters, as you can see,
One bought a cookie; then there were three.

Three little quarters I'll share with you,
One bought a pack of gum; then there were two.

Two little quarters could make a lot of fun,
One bought a horse ride; then there was one.

One little quarter was all that I had,
I took it to the bank and now I am sad.

Pennies and Dimes (West and Cox)
With my pennies, nickels and dimes,
Being at the candy store is the best of times.

Sweet little treats I'm sure to find,
How will I ever make up my mind?

With a bag of treats and drink to sip,
The change goes to the bank with a deposit slip.

LITERACY RESOURCES—BOOK LIST

26 Letters and 99 Cents by Tana Hoban
Coin County: A Bank in a Book by Jim Talbot
If You Made a Million by David M. Schwartz

Cowboys and Cowgirls

LITERACY APPLICATION

Sentence Segmenting

Sentence segmenting is a more advanced concept for preschoolers, but can be taught by explaining what a sentence is. Segmenting a sentence is when children see that individual words make up a sentence. When the children see their oral stories written in sentence form and then count and clap out the words, it helps them to understand sentence segmenting.

LITERACY OBJECTIVES

Children will:

▶ begin to understand what a sentence is.

▶ become authors and illustrators as they create their own campfire stories.

▶ listen to each other's stories.

SPOTLIGHT WORDS

branding • chaps • "Giddy up" • horse shoeing • "Howdy" • lasso • prairie • ranch • range • round-up

MATERIALS

bandanas • bedrolls • boots • camp utensils • canteens • chaps • cowboy hats • guitars (cut out of cardboard) • logs for pretend fire • pots and pans • roasting sticks • rope • saddles on large classroom blocks • stick horses • tents • tin cups and plates

PROPS

▶ **Trail Maps**: (see page 190 in the Appendix).

SETTING UP

Set up your dramatic play area to look like a campsite out on the prairie or in the mountains. Help the children cut out stars and then tape them to the ceiling or hang them on strings. Make a pretend fire using logs and red and yellow paper. Put other logs around the fire for seating. If desired, an adult can play a guitar and sing or tell stories around the campfire. Or play cowboy music in the background. Set up the block area with large blocks to make pretend horses and, if available, add real saddles. Put out ropes, bags, trail maps, and canteens. Give the children large paper and crayons so they can create their own trail maps. For outdoor time, bring out stick horses and a horseshoe game. Children can bring their trail maps they've made and go on a trail ride.

OPEN-ENDED QUESTIONS

What do cowboys and cowgirls think about while lying under the stars?
What campfire story would you tell if you were a cowboy or cowgirl?
What could a cowboy or cowgirl do during the day?
How do cowboys and cowgirls take care of their horses?

MAKING BOOKS

▶ **(Child's name)'s Campfire Story** (individual book): Ask three or four children at a time to sit around the campfire and tell stories. Tape record each child's story, and then type or write one sentence per page to create a book. While the children are illustrating their books, point out that each page has a sentence on it. Ask the children to count out the words, and then clap out the sentence (for example, "the-horse-ran-fast"). This may be the first time that children are exposed to the concept of sentences. Emphasize that they are authors and illustrators as they share their books with others at circle time.

EXTENSION ACTIVITIES

1) Invite a cowboy or cowgirl to visit the classroom and teach cowboy lingo. If you don't know of any cowboys or cowgirls in your area, invite a storyteller from your local library to come in dressed as a cowboy/girl.

2) Invite someone you know who plays the guitar to come in and teach the children campfire songs.

Occupations

3) Arrange for a storyteller to visit the classroom at circle time.

4) Play the game of horseshoes and let the children tally their scores on scorecards.

LITERACY RESOURCES— SONGS, POEMS, AND FINGERPLAYS

Home on the Range (traditional)
Oh, give me a home where the buffalo roam,
Where the deer and the antelope play;
Where seldom is heard a discouraging word
And the skies are not cloudy all day.

Chorus:
Home, home on the range
Where the deer and the antelope play.
Where seldom is heard a discouraging word
And the skies are not cloudy all day.

How often at night when the heavens are bright
With the lights from the glittering stars,
Have I stood there amazed and asked as I gazed
If their glory exceeds that of ours.

Chorus

Where the air is so pure, the zephyrs so free,
The breezes so balmy and light,
That I would not exchange my home on the range
For all of the cities so bright.

Chorus

Oh, I love those wild flowers in this dear land of ours,
The curlew, I love to hear scream,
And I love the white rocks and the antelope flocks
That graze on the mountain tops green.

Chorus

LITERACY RESOURCES—BOOK LIST

Adam Sharp, London Calling by George Edward Stanley
Birthday Mice! by Bethany Roberts
Black Cowboy, Wild Horses: A True Story by Julius Lester
The Brave Cowboy by Joan Walsh Anglund
The Magic Boots by Scott Emerson
My 1st Book of Cowboy Songs by Dolly Moon (editor)

Mechanic

LITERACY APPLICATION

Identifying the First Letter of One's Name

It is very important to write and display the children's names in several places (for example, names on cubbies, nametags, name cards, sign-in sheets, and so on). The first letter that has real meaning and value to children is the first letter of their name. They often get excited when they see "their" letter in the environment and point it out. They will say, "There's my 'T'—that's my letter!" As they get older they begin to identify other letters in their names and to recognize them in their world. This is where children start to understand what letters represent. As the children play mechanic, they can write their names on their business cards, sign-in sheets, and name badges.

LITERACY OBJECTIVES

Children will:

▶ attempt writing using letter-like forms by writing names on business cards, nametags, and key chains.

▶ recognize that print has meaning.

▶ pretend to read environmental print by looking at car manuals.

SPOTLIGHT WORDS

broken • engine • fix • gas • hood • mechanic • oil • tires

MATERIALS

baseball caps • big shirts • car manuals • empty, clean oil bottles • hubcaps • keys • large blocks • overalls • "real" old car parts • steering wheels • stickers for name badges • tools

PROPS

▶ **Business Card:** Cut paper into 3" or 4" squares. Write "Car Mechanic" at the top, and leave a space for the child's name and address. Let the children fill them out and decorate as desired.

▶ **Key Chain (star):** Cut out small star shapes and punch a hole in the top.

SETTING UP

Arrange the different car parts in the block area. Put out dress-up clothes, manuals, and tools. Encourage the children to create a car or other vehicle with the blocks and different car parts. Then, prompt the children to take on different roles in the auto repair shop, such as the mechanic or the owner of the car. Have stickers available so the children can write name badges. Also, provide paper key chains, sign-in sheets, and business cards for the children to write their names on.

OPEN-ENDED QUESTIONS

How are noises made by cars different than noises made by trucks?
How do mechanics fix things?
How does a car work?
What makes a car engine run?

MAKING BOOKS

▶ **My Little Car** (class book): Draw a simple outline of a car on a piece of paper. Make copies of the car pattern and give one to each child. Ask the children to name their car using the same first letter of their name. (For example, Fred's Ford, Betty's Blue Bertha, or Sally's Speedy Shuttle.) Encourage the children to decorate their car as desired. After filling in the details of their cars using crayons or markers, they can add details such as glitter for headlights and toothpicks for windshield wipers. Attach the pages together to make a class book.

▶ **The Mechanic We All Know** (individual book): Write each of the following sentences on the bottom of separate sheets of paper:

This is the mechanic whom we all know.
He fixes our car so we can go.
He fixes the flat so it rolls just so.
He works on the wires so the lights will go.
He puts oil in the car when the pressure is low.
He adjusts the wipers so no streaks will show.
This is the mechanic who we all know,
He fixes our car so we can go.

Staple the pages together. Write "The Mechanic We All Know" by
_____ on the title page. Encourage the children to illustrate
the corresponding pages. Ask the children to write their
own name on the title page and on each
corresponding page. Emphasize the first letter of
their name.

EXTENSION ACTIVITIES

1) Bring in several different tools from home and put
   them in a bag. During circle
   time, let the children take turns
   pulling out one tool at a time.
   Talk about the names of the
   tools and how they are used. You
   could also have the children
   bring a tool from home and do
   the same thing.
2) Go on a field trip to see a mechanic, an oil
   change shop, or an emissions shop.

LITERACY RESOURCES—
SONGS, POEMS, FINGERPLAYS

Windshield Wiper
I'm a windshield wiper. (bend arm at elbow with fingers pointing up)
This is how I go. (move arm to left and right, pivoting at elbow)
Back and forth, back and forth, (continue back and forth motion)
In the rain and snow. (continue back and forth motion)

LITERACY RESOURCES--BOOK LIST

3 Pigs Garage by Peter Lippman
Go, Go, Go! by David Goldin
Junk Pile by Lady Borton
Me, Dad, and Number 6 by Dana Andrew Jennings
My Car by Byron Barton
Start Your Engines, A Countdown Book by Mark Todd

Home

Babies
Attending to Pictures: Pretending to Read

Car Wash
Phoneme Blending

Hair Care
Distinguishing Between Oral and Written Language

Birthday Party
Meaningful Reading and Writing

Baking Day
Print Has Practical Uses Such as Following Written Directions

Cleaning
Words Are Different Than Pictures

House
Writing Messages With Scribble Marks

Tea Party
Letter Knowledge: Peers' Names

Laundry Day
Print Conveys Meaning: Seeing Words in Their Environment

Babies

LITERACY APPLICATION

Attending to Pictures: Pretending to Read

Children who pretend to read in their preschool years are more likely to become successful readers as they move into grade school. By pretending to read, children learn that print is oral language and that words can represent pictures. When adults read to children on a daily basis, they promote pretending to read. They also encourage it by listening attentively and commenting appropriately. Although children are not really reading, they feel like readers when they pretend to read. Therefore, it is important to give the children many opportunities to pretend to read, such as reading to their baby dolls.

LITERACY OBJECTIVES

Children will:

◗ pretend to read to their baby dolls by attending to picture clues.
◗ develop good listening skills by listening to lullaby music.

SPOTLIGHT WORDS

babies • big • bottle • cradle • gentle • happy • love • lullaby • quiet • rattle • sad • small • soft

MATERIALS

baby clothes • baby toys • bibs • blankets • board books • bottles • cribs • diaper bag • diapers • dishes • empty formula cans • lullaby music • rattles • rocking chairs • spoons

PROPS

▶ **Baby Information Chart:** Write the following sentences on a piece of paper, big enough to fill the entire page. Make copies for each child.

> *When I was born…*
> *I weighed _____ lbs. _____ oz.*
> *I was _____ inches tall.*
> *I was born at _____.*
> *I was born on _____, _____.*
> *Something special: _____.*

When I was born…
I weighed __6__ lbs. __15__ oz.
I was __17__ inches tall.
I was born at __11:57 AM__
I was born on __September 23__
Something special __Everyone__
said I had my Daddy's nose.

SETTING UP

Put the baby props and materials in the dramatic play area. If desired, let the children use the sand and water table to bathe their baby dolls. Encourage the children to read a book to their baby dolls. Play lullaby music to set the mood.

OPEN-ENDED QUESTIONS

How does your baby feel when you _____?
How do you feel when there is too much noise?
How will you take care of your baby?
What can you do to make your baby feel happy?

MAKING BOOKS

▶ **When I Was Born** (class book):
Make one copy of the Baby Information Chart (see props) for each child in the class. On another piece of paper, write "Guess Who?" at the top and leave space for a photo. Send home both pages with each child and have the parents fill in the information on the chart and glue a baby photo of the child on the other page. Ask the children to draw pictures of themselves on the back of their photo pages and write their names. Compile the pages into a class book. The children can try to guess who each child is by looking at the baby photos.

EXTENSION ACTIVITIES

1) Ask the children to bring in their baby pictures from home and use them to make a display or bulletin board.
2) Let the children bring in their favorite baby books from home and share them with the class.
3) Place a measuring chart in your classroom and keep track of how much the children are growing.

Home

LITERACY RESOURCES—SONGS, POEMS, AND FINGERPLAYS

Our Baby (West and Cox)
Our baby has a little nose,
And on her feet, ten tiny toes.
Her hand will grab my finger tight,
While I sing to her each night.

Sweet Little Baby (West and Cox)
(Tune: "Rock-a-Bye, Baby")
Sweet little baby,
Mother loves you,
Snuggle and cuddle,
A little kiss too!

Turn out the light,
And close your eyes tight.
Mother will wake you,
When it is light.
(Sing again, replacing "mother" with "father," "sister," "auntie," or "grandmother.")

LITERACY RESOURCES—BOOK LIST

Guess How Much I Love You by Sam McBratney
I Love You, Little One by Nancy Tafuri
Little Tiger's Big Surprise by Julie Sykes
Peter's Chair by Ezra Jack Keats
Rosie's Babies by Martin Waddell
When I Was Little by Jamie Lee Curtis

Car Wash

LITERACY APPLICATION

Phoneme Blending

Phonological awareness occurs when children become aware of the sounds within words. Support children as they explore and play with sounds in oral language, and help children connect their understanding of sounds to letters and words. Playing with sounds and words is a good way for children to begin to hear the different sounds within words, such as "apple," "bapple," and "snapple." In the car wash, the children will make sounds such as 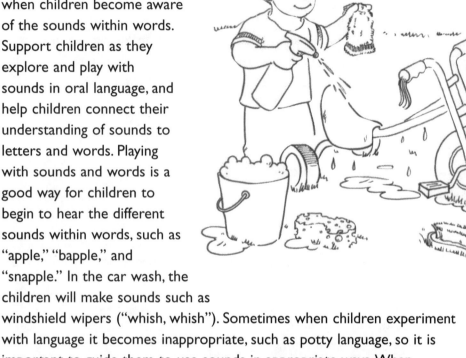 windshield wipers ("whish, whish"). Sometimes when children experiment with language it becomes inappropriate, such as potty language, so it is important to guide them to use sounds in appropriate ways. When children are allowed to play with these sounds, they connect literacy to everyday language and are more likely to succeed in reading.

LITERACY OBJECTIVES

Children will:

◗ begin to identify words that start with the same auditory sounds.
◗ understand the meaning of print by making signs.

SPOTLIGHT WORDS

clean • dirty • dry • in • out • rub • scrub • shine • spots • squeeze • squirt • vacuum • wash • wax • wet

MATERIALS

buckets • scrubbers • signs • sponges • spray bottles • towels • wax boxes

PROPS

▶ **Signs:** Make signs with the following words on them: "In," "Out," "Open," and "Closed."

SETTING UP

You can choose to have your car wash outside and use real soap and water to wash the children's tricycles, or you can have a pretend car wash inside. Encourage the children to make the sounds of the car wash as they are playing, for example, windshield wipers—whish, whish; vacuum—vroom, vroom; and spray—sss, sss. Let the children make their own signs for the car wash, such as: Car Wash $5, Open, Closed, Free, Drive Forward, or Wax. As needed, write down the words the children want on their signs so they can copy them.

OPEN-ENDED QUESTIONS

How are these two cars alike?
How are they different?

MAKING BOOKS

▶ **Wash and Go!** (class book): Give each child a page with the following poem typed on it:

> In a dusty, dirty car I drive
> Soon at the car wash I arrive.
> Clink, clank, clink, the money goes.
> Water spraying out of the hose.
> Pick up a brush to scrub-a-dub,
> Then with a rag I buff, polish, and rub.

Ask each child to describe a different kind of car that she would like to have go through the car wash. Then write it on her page with the sound it would make. Ask the children to draw their cars on their individual pages. Staple the title page and individual pages together to make a book.

EXTENSION ACTIVITIES

1) During circle time, help the children hear words that start with the same sound and then encourage them to create their own. For example: creaky, cranky car; wild wipers; very vital vacuum; wiping windows; swell swishing; silly suds; whistling water; and so on.
2) Let your class wash the school bus or van.
3) Take clipboards to a parking lot and ask the children to tally the different colors of cars.

LITERACY RESOURCES— SONGS, POEMS, AND FINGERPLAYS

The Wheels on the Car (West and Cox)
(Tune: "The Wheels on the Bus")
The wheels on the car go 'round and 'round,
Round and 'round, 'round and 'round.
The wheels on the car go 'round and 'round,
As we drive to the car wash in town.

2nd verse: The water on the car goes ssss, ssss, ssss…
3rd verse: The brushes on the car go scrub, scrub, scrub…
4th verse: The air on the car goes whoosh, whoosh, whoosh…
5th verse: The vacuum on the car goes vroom, vroom, vroom…

The car comes out and shine, shine, shines,
Shine, shine, shines; shine, shine, shines.
The car comes out and shine, shine, shines,
And looking, oh, so fine.

The Car Wash (West and Cox)
A dirty car I drive,
To the car wash we arrive.

"Clink, clank, clink" the money goes
As water sprays out of the hose.

Pick up a brush to scrub-a-dub-dub
Then with a rag I rub, rub, rub.

Swish, swash, spray it clean.
It's the shiniest car I've seen.

Driving home we hit some mud
Onto the window a great big thud.

OH, NO!
Back to the car wash we must go.

LITERACY RESOURCES—BOOK LIST

Car Wash by Sandra Steen
Dad's Car Wash by Harry A. Sutherland
The Scrubbly-Bubbly Car Wash by Irene O'Garden
Slugger's Car Wash by Stuart J. Murphy

. . . . Home . . . .

Hair Care

LITERACY APPLICATION

Distinguishing Between Oral and Written Language

It is important for children to be in an environment where they can learn to distinguish between oral and written language. In order to help children with this concept, give them many opportunities to talk and write. Providing children with experiences to talk, such as conversations, describing events, talking about their daily routines, and giving and following instructions will help build language skills. When children write on business cards, make appointments, take phone messages, and make signs, they see that oral language also can be written. Both oral and written language need to be a natural part of their play.

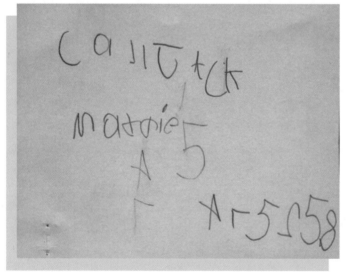

LITERACY OBJECTIVES

Children will:
- learn to ask questions for information as they take on the roles of hair designer and patron.
- practice writing on business cards and appointment books.
- have opportunities to have conversations.

SPOTLIGHT WORDS

barber • braid • brush • comb • dark • designer • down • gel • light • long • perm • salon • shampoo • short • thick • thin • up

MATERIALS

appointment book • bows • brushes • clips • combs • cordless broken curling iron • cup • dolls, • empty shampoo and gel bottles • hair apron • hair designer magazines • mirror • old cordless hair dryer • pencils • plastic curlers • shaver brush • shaver without blade • squirt bottles • Styrofoam heads • wigs

Safety Note: Never allow the children to do each other's hair—it can be a health hazard. Lice spread easily. Always provide Styrofoam heads with wigs or dolls for the children to use in this activity.

PROPS

▶ **Business Cards:** Make hair stylist business cards on index cards cut in half. Write "Hair Stylist" at the top, and leave a space for the child's name. The children can decorate them as desired.

▶ **Appointment Page:** Write "Appointments" at the top of a piece of paper. Write "Day _____" underneath. Then make a list of times: 10:00, 11:00, and so on, leaving a space for children to write names. Make copies of the page.

SETTING UP

Set up your dramatic play area to look like a hair salon. Put out the hair care props and materials. Include an appointment book for the children to write names on. Put out magazines for the patrons to read while they are waiting for their turns. Have business cards available for the children to write their names on and give to the other children.

OPEN-ENDED QUESTIONS

How would you like your hair done?
What do you want your hair to look like?
Why does your hair grow?

Home

MAKING BOOKS

▶ **My Hair** (individual book): Cut paper into large ovals and give one to each child. Put out collage materials such as curly craft hair, straw, or different colors of yarn. Encourage the children to draw a face and glue hair on it. Tape a tongue depressor on the back of the oval. Set up a puppet stage and let the children create stories with their puppets. Ask the children to dictate their stories as you write them down.

▶ **Hair** (class book): Ask the children to draw what they would like their hair to look like. If desired, use collage materials again. As the children describe their hair, write down their words. Make a title page and staple the pages together.

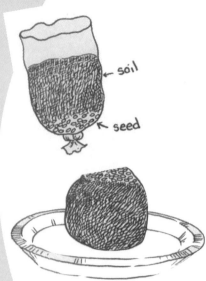

soil

seed

EXTENSION ACTIVITIES

1) Tell the children about "Locks of Love," which is a non-profit organization that provides hairpieces to financially disadvantaged children suffering from long-term medical hair loss.

2) Make grass hair heads using nylon socks. Cut the foot off an old nylon sock. (Use the footless part for this activity.) Tie one end of the sock. Place grass seed inside the bottom of the sock (where it is tied off), and then put soil over the seeds. Tie the other end in a knot, turn it over, and put it on a tray. Make sure to keep the soil moist. When the grass grows long enough, let the children give it a haircut with their scissors. If you want, the children can make funny faces on their heads for fun.

LITERACY RESOURCES—
SONGS, POEMS, AND FINGERPLAYS

Hair (West and Cox)
(Tune: "Did You Ever See a Lassie?")
Have you ever seen a hairdresser, hairdresser, hairdresser?
Have you ever seen a hairdresser do hair like this?
You wash it and cut it, you brush it and curl it.
Have you ever seen a hairdresser do hair like this?

Have you ever seen a hairdresser, hairdresser, hairdresser?
Have you ever seen a hairdresser do hair like this?
You rat it, you braid it, you crimp it, and glitz it.
Have you ever seen a hairdresser do hair like this?

Have you ever seen a hairdresser, hairdresser, hairdresser?
Have you ever seen a hairdresser do hair like this?
You perm it and dye it, you wrap it and dread it.
Have you ever seen a hairdresser do hair like this?

Have you ever had your hair go this way and that way
Have you ever had your hair go this way and that?
It goes in and out and over and under.
You will need a hairdresser to fix your hair nice.

Fuzzy Wuzzy Was a Bear (traditional)
Fuzzy Wuzzy was a bear.
Fuzzy Wuzzy had no hair.
Fuzzy Wuzzy wasn't fuzzy,
Was he?

LITERACY RESOURCES—BOOK LIST

Bad Hair Day by Susan Hood

Baghead by Jarrett J. Krosoczka

Bintou's Braids by Sylviane A. Diouf

Cowardly Clyde by Bill Peet

Franny B. Kranny, There's a Bird in Your Hair! by Harriet Lerner

Haircuts at Sleepy Sam's by Michael R. Strickland

Happy to Be Nappy by Bell Hooks

Harriet's Horrible Hair Day by Dawn Lesley Stewart

Hats Off to Hair by Virginia Kroll

I Love My Hair by Natasha Anastasia Tarpley

Moosetache by Margie Palatini

Nappy Hair by Carolivia Herron

Birthday Party

LITERACY APPLICATION

Meaningful Reading and Writing

Appropriate activities that incorporate writing and reading support the development of emergent literacy. Formal worksheets are inappropriate because they are abstract and often have little meaning and application to children. Requiring children to do a sit-down formal literacy activity can stifle their development.

However, when children create birthday cards and invitations, they are motivated to write because it is a meaningful, real-life situation. They are excited to give their cards to others and play out roles. Appropriate activities invite children to expand upon their writing skills at their own pace, and dramatic play provides real reasons to use writing and reading.

LITERACY OBJECTIVES

Children will:

▸ recognize and read some words as they make birthday cards and invitations.

▸ identify words that rhyme as they play games.

SPOTLIGHT WORDS

birthday • card • excitement • friends • gift • invitation • party favor • surprise • wishes

MATERIALS

boxes for presents • candles • foam cake • games (such as Pin the Tail on the Donkey) • Happy Birthday signs • name cards • napkins and paper plates • party bags • party favors • party hats • streamers • wrapping paper

PROPS

▶ **Birthday Cards:** Use squares of paper, cardstock, or index cards. Write "Happy Birthday" on the front and write "To:" and "From:" on the back. Let the children decorate them.

▶ **Birthday Party Invitation:** Use squares of paper, cardstock, or index cards. Write "You're Invited to a Birthday Party" on the front and Time: ____, Day: ____, and Place:_____ on the back.

SETTING UP

Help the children make a large "Happy Birthday" sign on butcher paper. Put the birthday props in the dramatic play area. Encourage the children to make decorations and signs. Let the children make birthday cards and invitations for their classmates. Write down the names of the children on name cards for them to copy, if needed. If desired, have a place in the art area for the children to make presents and wrap them. Help the children take turns being the birthday girl or boy.

OPEN-ENDED QUESTIONS

What is a wish?
Why are birthdays important to you?
How do others feel at a birthday party?

MAKING BOOKS

▶ **Our Friends** (class book): Cut poster board or cardstock into 4" x 8" pieces and tape them together with wide, clear tape on the back. Fold the pages back and forth to make an accordion-style book. Make a body pattern by drawing an outline of a body, similar to a gingerbread man shape, about 5" tall. Make copies of the body pattern and cut them out. Take close-up photographs of the children's faces and glue one child's face to each body pattern. Encourage the children to draw their clothes on their own body pattern. Glue one finished body pattern to each page in the accordion book. Then, record the nice things that children say about each other on each page. Make sure each child has something written on his or her page. This is very meaningful to children.

EXTENSION ACTIVITIES

1) Explain to the children what an Un-Birthday is (a day to pretend it is your birthday). Read or watch the part in "Alice in Wonderland" about Un-Birthdays.

2) Let the children help make cupcakes and decorate them.

3) Play birthday party games that help the children recognize rhyming words. For example, draw or glue pictures of words that are easy to rhyme onto strips of paper. Divide the children into groups, with one adult per group. Pull out a strip of paper from a hat and let the children come up with different rhyming words for it. The adult with the group records their words on a small chalkboard or dry-erase board. Set a timer, and the group with the most rhyming words when time's up helps the other groups. For added fun, make nonsense words count!

LITERACY RESOURCES— SONGS, POEMS, AND FINGERPLAYS

Five Birthday Presents (West and Cox)
Five birthday presents sitting on the floor.
I opened the big one, now there are four.
Four birthday presents just for me.
I opened the long one, now there are three.
Three birthday presents all from you.
I opened the red one, now there are two.
Two birthday presents, oh, this is fun.
I opened the flat one, now there is one.
One birthday present all wrapped up tight.
I tore it open with all my might!

Today Is a Birthday! (West and Cox)
Today is a birthday,
I wonder for whom?
We know it's somebody
Who's right in this room.
So look all around you
For somebody who
Is laughing and smiling
My goodness—it's you!

LITERACY RESOURCES—BOOK LIST

The Secret Birthday Message by Eric Carle
The Seven Silly Eaters by Mary Ann Hoberman

Baking Day

LITERACY APPLICATION

Print Has Practical Uses Such as Following Written Directions

It is important for children to understand the function of print. When children see adults following directions they see how print is used. They learn that following a sequence is important. As children look at recipes and recipe books while they pretend to bake, they develop a sense of order and see that print has practical uses. As children dictate recipes that adults record, they gain an understanding of the meaning of print, which is a crucial part of learning to read.

LITERACY OBJECTIVES

Children will:
▶ understand the function of print by looking at recipes.
▶ carry out a series of directions while using recipes.
▶ learn creative writing skills when making a recipe book.
▶ take turns with others.
▶ be exposed to different cultural foods.

SPOTLIGHT WORDS

bake • bakery • beat • bitter • cook • crisp • fry • hard • ingredients • knead • lumpy • measure • mix • recipe • runny • sift • soft • sour • stir • sweet

MATERIALS

aprons • blank recipe cards • bowls • cookie cutters • cookie sheets • hot pads • muffin tins • pencils • pizza pans • plastic tablecloth • playdough • recipe cards books • rolling pins • small baking pans • spatulas • spoons • whisks

PROPS

1) Recipe cards (see page 188 in the Appendix): Make copies of this page and cut out the recipe cards.

SETTING UP

Put the baking equipment in the dramatic play area. If using playdough, place a plastic tablecloth on the floor for easy cleanup. Have recipe cards and books easily accessible for the children to look at. Encourage the children to make up their own recipes and write them on blank cards. If desired, bring the sand and water table into the dramatic play area to expand this activity.

OPEN-ENDED QUESTIONS

What do we need to make a _____?

MAKING BOOKS

▶ **Our Family's Favorite Recipes** (individual book): Send home a recipe card (see props) with each child and ask the parents to use black ink to write down their family's favorite recipe. After the children bring in their recipe cards, ask them how they would make the recipe. Write down their responses on another piece of paper. Glue the recipe card to the page with the child's version. Make copies of all the pages so that each child has all of them. Attach the pages together to make a book for each child. These are great to give as a gift!

EXTENSION ACTIVITIES

1) Let the children help you make something from a simple recipe of your choice. Enlarge the recipe on a piece of poster board so that all of the children can see and follow it with you. If desired, take the children on a field trip to the grocery store the day before to buy the ingredients.

2) Role play "The Little Red Hen." Talk about how important it is for everyone to do his or her part.

3) Help teach children to share by making a cake and then starting to eat it by yourself. Refuse to share with the children when they ask. (This will encourage a discussion about how it feels when others don't share and help the children to come up with a resolution to the problem.) In the end, share the cake with everyone and discuss the importance of sharing in your classroom.

Baking (West and Cox)
Sift it,
Sift it,
Yum, yum, yum.
I can't wait
Till the cookies are done.

Mix it,
Mix it,
Yum, yum, yum,
Count the chocolate chips,
One by one.

Roll it,
Roll it,
Yum, yum, yum,
Onto the cookie sheet,
Hot as the sun.

Bake it,
Bake it,
Yum, yum, yum,
Cookies are rising,
They're almost done.

Eat it,
Eat it,
Yum, yum, yum,
This has really been,
So much fun.

The Baker (West and Cox)
The baker is ready to make
A big double-layered pink cake.
With flour and spice
And everything nice.
Into the oven to bake.

The baker is ready to roll,
Ingredients go in the bowl.
The dough, he rolls out,
That's what it's about.
Now all our tummies are full.

Home

LITERACY RESOURCES—BOOK LIST

Bread, Bread, Bread by Ann Morris

If You Give a Mouse a Cookie by Laura Joffe Numeroff

If You Give a Moose a Muffin by Laura Joffe Numeroff

Jake Baked the Cake by B.G. Hennessy

The Little Red Hen by Lucinda McQueen

Pancakes, Pancakes! by Eric Carle

Rice by Pam Robson

Stone Soup by Ann McGovern

Cleaning

LITERACY APPLICATION

Words Are Different Than Pictures

Lists and charts with pictures and text help children understand that the print is telling what the picture represents. Children begin to read by associating pictures with words. Create a list or chart using children's ideas, such as the items they are going to clean. Then, accompany the text with pictures so the children will associate each word with a picture.

LITERACY OBJECTIVES

Children will:

▶ read environmental print by looking at labels.

▶ demonstrate an understanding of the function of print by making lists or charts.

SPOTLIGHT WORDS

broom • clean • custodian • disinfectant • dust • dustpan • germs • maid • mop • scouring pad • soap • sponge

MATERIALS

aprons • bandanas • buckets • charts • empty, thoroughly washed cleaning product containers • dust pans • empty soap bottles • feather dusters • mops • paper • pencils • rags • rubber gloves • scouring pads • small brooms • sponges • spray bottles

PROPS

▶ **Cleaning Chart:** Make a chart entitled "Cleaning Chart" and divide the page into two columns. Write "Name" at the top of the left-hand column and "Job" at the top of the right-hand column.

1. Sweep the floor.
2. Dust the table.
3. Wash the mirror.
4. Take out trash.

☆ CLEANING CHART ☆

Name	Job
Meghan	dust bookshelves
Caleb	wash dishes
José	clean mirrors
Alexis	clean hamster cage
Clay	mop floor
Darla	take out trash

SETTING UP

Put the cleaning props in the dramatic play area. Provide a variety of cleaning containers with labels for the children to look at. Help the children make a chart or list of the things they are going to clean. Allow the children, when possible, to write the words or draw the pictures themselves.

OPEN-ENDED QUESTIONS

Why is it important to keep things clean?
Where do germs grow?

MAKING BOOKS

▶ **Rub-a-Dub-Dub, the Things I Scrub** (individual book): Ask the children to draw pictures and write or dictate the things that they would like to clean. Make sure the words are under the pictures they represent.

EXTENSION ACTIVITIES

1) Talk about poison safety and the symbol for poison.
2) Talk about germs. Go on a "germ hunt" in your classroom. Encourage the children to guess where they might find germs. Then, have each child touch a surface with one finger and then press the finger in a petri dish. Label the dishes with the surface and child's name. Let the germs grow for a few days, and then encourage the children to compare the different bacteria that have grown.
3) With the children's help, record their ideas to make a cleaning list, picnic list, grocery list, and favorite ice cream chart. Children can either draw pictures of each item or cut out pictures from magazines.

LITERACY RESOURCES— SONGS, POEMS, AND FINGERPLAYS

I Like to Clean My Room (West and Cox)
I like to clean my room each day,
Before I go outside to play.
I hang up my shirt,
And vacuum the dirt.
And now I'm all through—
HURRAY!

Clean-Up Time (traditional)

Clean-up time,
Clean-up time,
Time to stop
And end our play.

Clean-up time,
Clean-up time,
Time to put
Our toys away.

LITERACY RESOURCES—BOOK LIST

Five Little Monkeys With Nothing to Do by Eileen Christelow
Mrs. Wishy Washy by Joy Cowley
Mud by Mary Lyn Ray
Wishy Washy Farm by Joy Cowley

House

Writing messages helps children understand that writing is a way of communicating, and children enjoy writing and receiving messages and notes from each other. Having a special place and tool to write with creates a desire to read and write. Therefore, use a variety of writing tools to stimulate interest in writing, such as chalk, markers, dry-erase markers, colored pencils, Post-It notes, lined paper, notebooks, colorful notepads, and different shapes of paper. Message boards posted in the housekeeping area also provide children with opportunities to write messages to and from each other. Encourage children to write at any level. Separate scribble marks are an important part of the writing continuum.

LITERACY OBJECTIVES

Children will:
▶ understand the purpose of print.
▶ practice writing on message boards and "to do" lists.

SPOTLIGHT WORDS

adopted • apartment • aunt • baby • brother • condo • cottage • cousin • duplex • family • father • flat • foster family • grandma • grandpa • home • love • mother • ranch • sister • stepdad • stepmom • townhouse • uncle

MATERIALS

books • dishes • dolls • dress-up clothes • dry-erase markers • junk mail • love notes • pencils • plastic food • Post-It notes

PROPS

▶ **Message Board:** Decorate the borders of a piece of plain paper. Write "Message Board" at the top.

▶ **"To Do" List:** On the top of a piece of paper or chart paper, write "Things I Have to Do!" Draw lines on the page to look like list paper.

SETTING UP

Keep your dramatic play area set up like a house. Make sure the area has dress-up clothes, dishes, and plastic food. Add literacy props such as junk mail, message boards, and "to do" lists and encourage the children to write lists or notes. When asked, help the children with their writing.

OPEN-ENDED QUESTIONS

Where are you going?

What are you doing today?

What could he/she do?

Who could you get to play with you?

Who would you like to be?

MAKING BOOKS

▶ **Our Families** (class book): Ask the children to draw their families and label the pictures. Encourage all forms of writing, including scribble marks. Collect the pages and staple them together.

▶ **These Are the People Who Live in My House** (individual book): Talk about the different things that children do in their houses. Give each child a few pieces of construction paper or cardstock. Ask the children to label and illustrate the outside of their houses on one piece of paper and the inside of their houses on the rest of the paper. For example, the child could label and draw different rooms or levels of his house on different pages. Staple the papers together on one side to make the pages of the book. Help each child cut out a triangle and staple it to the top of the last page to make the roof of the house. Encourage all forms of writing, including scribble marks.

Home

EXTENSION ACTIVITIES

1) Ask the children to bring in a family picture. Let them share and talk about the members of their families.

2) Help the children write love notes to a member of their family and then send them in the mail.

3) Teach the children about different kinds of families and homes, for example: stepfamilies and foster families, and apartments, duplexes, condos, cottages, and brick homes.

LITERACY RESOURCES— SONGS, POEMS, AND FINGERPLAYS

Here Is a House*

Here is a house, built up high (stretch arms up and touch fingertips like a roof)
With two tall chimneys, reaching the sky. (stretch arms up separately)
Here is the window. (make a square shape with your hands)
Here is the door. (knock)
If we peep inside, we'll see a family of four. (wiggle four fingers)
* Adapted from traditional

Grandpa or Grandma's Glasses (traditional)

These are Grandpa's glasses. (make glasses with fingers)
This is Grandpa's hat. (tap head)
This is how he folds his hands, (fold hands)
And puts them in his lap. (place hands in lap)

LITERACY RESOURCES—BOOK LIST

Guess How Much I Love You by Sue McBratney
I Love You, Little One by Nancy Tafuri
I Love You, Stinky Face by Lisa McCourt
Love You Forever by Robert Munsch
Mama, Do You Love Me? by Barbara M. Josse
Who's in a Family? by Robert Skutch

Tea Party

LITERACY APPLICATION

Letter Knowledge—Peers' Names

Once children have learned to recognize and write their own names, they naturally become interested and excited about learning the names of family members and peers. Learning others' names is an excellent way for children to expand their knowledge of letters and print. Put the names of all the children in several places in the classroom so they can see their peers' names in print. The children are learning that words are made up of letters. Let them write their peers' names on invitations and thank-you notes, providing them with a purpose to read and write.

LITERACY OBJECTIVES

Children will:

▶ have a purpose to write by writing invitations, seating cards, and thank-you notes.

▶ understand the purpose of print.

▶ learn to read and write their peers' names on invitations.

SPOTLIGHT WORDS

cup • etiquette • hospitality • hostess • invitation • "May I?" • please • R.S.V.P. • tarts • teapot • thank you • saucer

MATERIALS

dolls • fake jewelry • hats • invitations • markers • name cards • party dresses • pencils • placemats • plastic tea set • tablecloth • thank-you notes • trays

PROPS

▸ **Invitations:** On a piece of paper, write "Come to Tea With Me" at the top. Write the following items on the rest of the page:

Day _____
Please arrive at _____
Place _____
Type of Tea _____
R.S.V.P.

Let the children decorate the invitations as desired.

▸ **Thank-You Notes:** Fold a piece of plain paper in half. Write "Thank You" in large letters on the outside of one half (like a card). Let the children decorate them.

SETTING UP

Let the children make plans for a tea party. Encourage them to make invitations for their friends. Put the tea party props in the housekeeping area. Help the children make seating cards and placemats to use at their party. Let them use name cards from which to copy their classmates' names. Encourage the children to invite different friends to their tea party and write thank-you notes afterwards.

OPEN-ENDED QUESTIONS

What kind of plans do you need to make for the tea party?
Who could you invite?
What shall we serve at the tea party?
When shall we have the tea party?
Who will host our party?

MAKING BOOKS

▸ **A Tea Party for Me** (individual book): Encourage the children to draw pictures and write the names of the children they would like to come to their tea party. Staple the pages together to make a book.

EXTENSION ACTIVITIES

1) Talk about different kinds of fancy food to have at a tea party, such as tarts, finger sandwiches, and hors d'oeuvres.
2) Tell the children about different countries that have tea parties.
3) Teach the children about good manners and etiquette.
4) Have the children make their own placemats for their tea party. Encourage them to write their friends' names and draw pictures on the mats.

LITERACY RESOURCES—
SONGS, POEMS, AND FINGERPLAYS

Tea Time (West and Cox)
There is a neighbor of mine,
Who likes to serve tea all the time.
She makes fancy tarts
In the shape of small hearts.
We'll join her at quarter to nine.

Queen of Hearts*
The Queen of Hearts,
She made some tarts,
All on a summer's day;
The King of Hearts,
Called for the tarts,
And ate them all that day.
*Adapted from traditional

LITERACY RESOURCES—BOOK LIST

The Best Tea Party Ever by Sonali Fry
Let's Have a Tea Party by Emilie Barnes
Miss Spider's Tea Party by David Kirk

Laundry Day

LITERACY APPLICATION

Print Conveys Meaning, Seeing Words in Their Environment

It is important to teach children to see the words that are in their environment. As children become aware of print in their everyday world, they begin to understand that reading and writing are ways for them to gain information, create ideas, and increase their knowledge. For example, when a child discovers a word or label on a shirt, or directions (such as in the laundry props), she gets excited and wants to share that word with others. Not only does the child discover the word, but her enthusiasm helps her peers look closely at print. When children recognize words, they are taking a major step toward reading.

LITERACY OBJECTIVES

Children will:

▶ begin to see words in their environment.
▶ identify words that start with the same auditory sound.
▶ create their own book.

SPOTLIGHT WORDS

clean • clothesline • clothespins • dirty • dry • dryer • hang • iron • laundry • rinse • scrub • soak • soap • washer • wet

MATERIALS

baskets • child-sized ironing boards • clothesline • clothespins • empty laundry soap containers • old baby clothes • old T-shirts • pretend washer and dryer (made from boxes) • small laundry baskets • wooden irons

PROPS

▶ **Laundry Soap Instructions:** Make a chart showing the steps in washing clothes. Include sorting by color, temperature (hot water, warm water, or cold water) and how much soap to measure.

SETTING UP

Add a pretend washer and dryer to your dramatic play area. (You can make them out of large boxes, if needed.) Set up ironing boards and a clothesline. Put out other laundry props. Make sure there are words on the shirts that you use as "dirty clothes." Put out several different colors of laundry baskets for sorting, and attach labels such as "colors" and "whites." Collect several laundry detergent containers and cut out the directions. Encourage the children to look for the words hot, warm, or cold on the detergent labels. Give the children blank pieces of paper to write the words and display them on the washing machines.

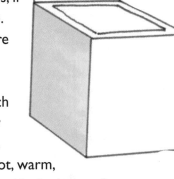
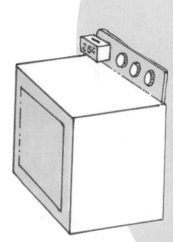

OPEN-ENDED QUESTIONS

How will you get your clothes clean?
How does a washing machine get clothes clean?
Why do we need to clean our clothes?
What word can you see on this T-shirt?
How many words can you see on this box (label, shirt, and so on)?

MAKING BOOKS

▶ **Katie Kosh Hangs Up Her Wash** (class book): Read the story *Mrs. McNosh Hangs Up Her Wash* by Sarah Weeks. Ask the children to bring a laundry soap label and directions from home. Help the children glue their label and directions to the title page of the book. Then, give each child a piece of paper cut into a shirt shape. Ask the children to write what they would hang on a clothesline and draw it on their page. Staple all of the pages together at the shoulder of the shirt pattern, and then slip two tiny clothespins over the staples. Thread a piece of yarn through the clothespins to make it look like it is on a clothesline.

EXTENSION ACTIVITIES

1) Read the book *Mrs. Wishy Washy* and talk about all of the different things we need to keep clean. Point out the words that start with the same auditory sound and encourage the children to come up different ones (for example, stained shirts, dirty denim, or painted pants).

2) Let the children role play the story of *Mrs. Wishy Washy*. Encourage the children to take on the roles of the different characters in the book and then present it to another class or to their parents.

LITERACY RESOURCES— SONGS, POEMS, AND FINGERPLAYS

Ten Little Socks (West and Cox)
Ten little socks hanging on the line,
One blew off, now there are nine.
Nine little socks hanging by the gate,
One flew away, now there are eight.
Eight little socks wave up to heaven,
One fell down, now there are seven.
Seven little socks hung between two sticks,
One blew away and now there are six.
Six little socks dancing alive,
One slipped off, now there are five.
Five little socks hung high above the floor,
One was knocked off and now there are four.
Four little socks as high as a tree,
One got stuck and now there are three.
Three little socks, all clean and new,
One disappeared and now there are two.
Two little socks drying in the sun,
One's faded so it's really just one.
One little sock left hanging on the line,
Let's take it down, it's probably mine.

LITERACY RESOURCES—BOOK LIST

The Day Jimmy's Boa Ate the Wash by Trinka Hakes Noble
Mrs. McNosh Hangs Up Her Wash by Sarah Weeks
Mrs. Wishy Washy by Joy Cowley

Nature

Fishing
Letter Knowledge: Identifying Letters

Beach
Retelling Stories Using Verbal and Narrative Skills

Picnic
Writing Letters

Camping
Sequencing

Fishing

LITERACY APPLICATION

Letter Knowledge: Identifying Letters

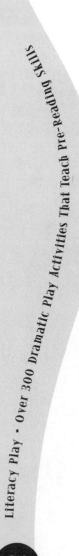

Letters taught in isolation teach children letters but not their purpose. Teaching children to recognize letters should be a component of a literacy program, but not the only focus. It is appropriate to expose children to letters by having magnetic letters, manipulative letters, sandpaper letters, letter molds, letter stencils, letter cards, letter stamps, and laminated alphabet sheets available. When children fish for letters in this dramatic play area, they can practice identifying letters. It is important to encourage the children to explore letters and manipulate them into words as they are ready.

LITERACY OBJECTIVES

Children will:

▶ identify and name some letters on paper fish.

▶ generate different options for writing a story.

▶ dictate their thoughts and stories with anticipation that they will be written.

SPOTLIGHT WORDS

angler • catch and release • fishing pole • hooks • net • tackle box • stream • waders

MATERIALS

blue tarp (for stream) • boat (if desired) • boots • buckets • fishing poles • hats • nets • paper fish or stuffed fish made from fabric • tackle box • vests • yarn • worms

PROPS

▶ **Fish Pattern** (see page 189 in the Appendix): Use the pattern to cut out a variety of paper fish. Write letters, words with pictures, or children's names on the fish. Attach a safety pin or paper clip to the mouth of each one. Laminating the fish will help them last longer.

▶ **Fishing License:** On index cards, write "Fishing License" at the top, and leave a space for the child's name and expiration date. Decorate it with a picture of a fish.

Fishing License

name _____

expires _____

SETTING UP

Cut a long, narrow piece of blue tarp, about 3' wide, to use for the stream. Put out the fishing materials and props. Make fishing poles by attaching string to dowels and tying magnets to the ends of the strings. Round magnets with a hole in the center will last longer. Encourage the children to fish for the letters that are familiar to them, such as those in their names. Encourage the children to write their names on their own fishing licenses.

OPEN-ENDED QUESTIONS

Which fish do you think will taste the best if we cooked it?
Do you think the stream gets crowded for the fish?

MAKING BOOKS

▶ **Fish Tale** (class or individual book): Cut out the fish pattern (see page 189 in the Appendix). Make one for each child in the class. Encourage the children to name their fish with a letter of the alphabet. For example, "My fish Abby starts with an A." Then, let the children create a story about their fish (on the back of the fish). Connect the fish pages with a ring and attach a piece of string. Make a fishing pole with a dowel or stick. Tie the string to the dowel and cover with tape so it is secure.

EXTENSION ACTIVITIES

1) Make fish of different lengths and let the children measure them with a ruler or measuring tape.
2) Talk about different kinds of fish. Show the children a poster or book with pictures of different fish. Then, let the children draw and paint their own fish to catch.
3) Make different kinds of paper fish to meet the needs of the children. For example, write different words, names of children, or numerals on the fish. You can also create a matching game. For example, match the fish with three dots to the fish with the numeral 3, and so on.

LITERACY RESOURCES—
SONGS, POEMS, AND FINGERPLAYS

I'm a Little Fishy (West and Cox)
(Tune: "I'm a Little Teapot")
I'm a little fishy, I can swim.
Here is my tail, here is my fin.
When I want to have fun with my friend,
I wiggle my tail and dive right in.

Ice Fishing (West and Cox)
I went ice fishing
And took my pole.
I sunk my hook
In a little hole.

My teeth were chattering
My fingers were numb.
I was beginning to think
That this was dumb.

The little brown worm
Began to wiggle.
When at last
I felt a jiggle.

My heart skipped a beat
When my pole did tug.
Then my dad jumped up
And gave me a hug.

LITERACY RESOURCES—BOOK LIST

Big Al by Andrew Clements
Fish Eyes: A Book You Can Count On by Lois Ehlert
Swimmy by Leo Lionni

Beach

LITERACY APPLICATION

Retelling Stories Using Verbal and Narrative Skills

Children practice verbal and narrative skills as they role play during dramatic play. When children interact with each other, they are exposed to new words that increase their vocabulary. Children develop purposeful narratives and scripts to match the roles they assume or are assigned to in their play at the beach. They use narrative and verbal skills, which are essential parts of reading comprehension.

LITERACY OBJECTIVES

Children will:

▶ respond with appropriate comments or questions about marine life after listening to text.

▶ recognize and name sounds from an ocean environment.

▶ write using alphabet-like letter forms while making signs.

SPOTLIGHT WORDS

coral • fins • mask • ocean • oxygen tank • regulator • sand • scuba diver • shells • snorkel

MATERIALS

beach balls • beach towels • beach umbrella • books about marine life • cassette tape or CD with ocean sounds • empty sunscreen bottles • flippers • hats • large blue tarp (ocean) • oxygen tank made from 2-liter bottle • paper and pencils for sign • plastic sea animals • sand toys (buckets, shovels, molds) • scuba masks • shells • sun visors • sunglasses

SETTING UP

Cut out a large oval from a blue tarp to be the ocean. Make an oxygen tank for scuba divers out of plastic 2-liter soda bottles. Spray paint the bottle gray and then attach duct tape straps. Lay the "ocean" on the floor and put out the beach materials. Place the shells and plastic sea animals on the tarp for the children to "dive" for. Listen to a tape with sounds of ocean waves, marine life, and seagulls to set the mood. Encourage the children to make signs such as "Warning," "No Swimming," "High Tide," and "Open."

OPEN-ENDED QUESTIONS

What kinds of fish live in warm water? Salty water? Cold water?
How many different fish live in the ocean?
What makes mammals different than fish?

MAKING BOOKS

▷ **The Beach** (individual book): Write each line of the following poem on separate pieces of paper:

> *Shimmering sands,*
> *Sand castles tall,*
> *Crashing waves,*
> *Tossing a ball.*
> *Seashell treasures,*
> *Seagulls call,*
> *Sunburned noses,*
> *Come one and all.*

Make enough copies so that each child has all of the pages. Encourage the children to illustrate the different pages of the poem as follows:

▷ Shimmering sands: Glue white sand on the page.
▷ Sand castles tall: Draw a sandcastle.
▷ Crashing waves: Mix different colors of blue watercolor paint.
▷ Tossing a ball: Cut a ball shape from construction paper and glue it to the page.
▷ Seashell treasures: Glue real seashell pieces to the page.
▷ Seagulls call: Glue white feathers to the page.
▷ Sunburned noses: Draw a red nose.
▷ Come one and all: Draw a picture of friends.

Do one page a day, so children aren't overwhelmed. After the children have completed their books, ask them to describe what is happening on each page. They can write this on the back of the previous page with help, if needed. Practice reading the poem each day so the children will learn to read it or memorize it.

EXTENSION ACTIVITIES

1) Prepare a display of different kinds of shells and coral on the science table for the children to examine with magnifying glasses.

2) Make sunglasses out of two connecting plastic rings from a six-pack holder, with pipe cleaners for the ear pieces. You can make colored lenses from cellophane.

3) Cut out sand buckets and shovels from construction paper. Make a matching game by placing pictures of marine life on shovels and clues on buckets. Encourage the children to find the right match.

LITERACY RESOURCES— SONGS, POEMS, AND FINGERPLAYS

Dolphins (West and Cox)
The dolphins swim near
One by one.
Their gray backs glistening
In the sun.

Sandcastles (West and Cox)
Buckets and shovels,
And my little hands
Will create castles
In the soft, wet sand.

LITERACY RESOURCES—BOOK LIST

Baby Beluga by Raffi
Commotion in the Ocean by Giles Andreae
A Dolphin's Tale by Richard R. Blake
Just Grandma and Me by Mercer Mayer
The Rainbow Fish by Marcus Pfister
Somewhere in the Ocean by Jennifer Ward and T.J. Marsh

Picnic

LITERACY APPLICATION

Writing Letters

When children create their own books, they are motivated to read and write. They are excited about reading their own books and will pretend to read them over and over. This also encourages them to do creative writing. To get them started, choose a book that is simple, easy to add to, and repetitive, for example, *It Looked Like Spilt Milk* by Charles G. Shaw or *Brown Bear, Brown Bear What Do You See?* by Bill Martin, Jr. and Eric Carle. After the children are familiar with the book, help them generate their own ideas. Then they will be ready to write their own stories. The children can dictate as you or another adult writes. Encourage the children to write letters as they create their stories. This increases their desire to write stories later. All children have stories to share, so it is important to give them opportunities to do creative writing.

LITERACY OBJECTIVES

Children will:

▶ create their own stories.

▶ write and match different words.

▶ demonstrate book awareness and appreciation.

▶ pretend to read by attending to picture clues on a picnic list.

SPOTLIGHT WORDS

basket • birds • clouds • cold • hot • insects • storms • sunny • warm • wet • windy

MATERIALS

basket • blanket • book bag • books • dress-up clothes • paper • paper cups • paper plates • pencils • plastic ants • plastic utensils • play food

PROPS

▶ **Picnic List With Pictures** (see page 193 in the Appendix): Make a copy of this picnic list for children to use, or make your own using this list as a model.

SETTING UP

Put the picnic props in a large open area of the classroom or outside. Encourage the children to use the picnic list when they gather items for their picnic. Place paper and pencils out for the children to add to the list. Encourage the children to pretend to read books at their picnic. Provide them with a bag of books that they are familiar with. After their play, let the children write their own stories.

OPEN-ENDED QUESTIONS

How do clouds move?
What do clouds look like to you?
Can clouds be different colors?
Do you hear birds singing? How many songs can you hear?

MAKING BOOKS

▶ **A Little Picnic** (individual book): Write the following two lines at the top of a piece of paper. Make enough copies so that each child will have a few pages.

A little picnic we will make,
In the basket we will take…

Brainstorm with the children all of the different things they could take on a picnic. Then, give the children the pages and encourage them to make their own book about what they would take. Let them write or dictate the words and then illustrate it. You may need to write the word first so the children can use it as a model. This will help them see the letters in their word when writing it in their books. Staple the pages together to make a book.

EXTENSION ACTIVITIES

1) Ask the children to create their own stories, for example, about their own picnic, a walk, or clouds. Read them a story such as *Teddy Bear's Picnic* by Jez Alborough, *I Went Walking* by Sue Williams, or *It Looked Like Spilt Milk* by Charles G. Shaw to get them thinking of ideas. Brainstorm all the different kinds of things they could do in their stories. Then, have the children individually dictate their stories to you.

Nature

2) Ask the children to bring a teddy bear from home to come to a "Teddy Bear Picnic." (Make sure you have a few extra teddy bears on hand in case someone forgets or doesn't have one.)

3) Let the children daydream outside and look at the clouds as you read *It Looked Like Spilt Milk* by Charles G. Shaw. Then ask the children to describe what they see in the clouds.

LITERACY RESOURCES— SONGS, POEMS, AND FINGERPLAYS

A Little Picnic (West and Cox)
A little picnic we will make.
Sandwiches, cookies we did bake,
All in the basket we will take
To play on the beach by the lake.

The Ants Go Marching One By One*
The ants go marching one by one, hurrah, hurrah.
The ants go marching one by one, hurrah, hurrah.
The ants go marching one by one,
The little one said, "Let's have some fun!"
And they all go marching down to the ground,
Where the worms crawl around.
Boom, Boom, Boom.

The ants go marching two by two....
...The little one stopped to tie his shoe.

The ants go marching three by three...
...The little one tried to tickle me.

The ants go marching four by four...
...The little one wants to play some more.

The ants go marching five by five...
...The little one says, "Let's get alive!"
* Adapted from traditional

LITERACY RESOURCES—BOOK LIST

Brown Bear, Brown Bear, What Do You See? by Bill Martin, Jr. and Eric Carle
In the Tall, Tall Grass by Denise Fleming
It's the Bear! by Jez Alborough
Let's Go Froggy! by Jonathan London
Lunch by Denise Fleming
My Friend Bear by Jez Alborough
Where's My Teddy? by Jez Alborough

Camping

LITERACY APPLICATION

Sequencing

Children need to learn to sequence a series of events, and they should be able to identify the beginning, middle, and end of a story. This will increase their reading comprehension. While camping, the children pretend to go on trail hikes. They must follow a map from the beginning to the end, and follow the order in sequence.

LITERACY OBJECTIVES

Children will:

▶ recognize and name sounds from the environment.
▶ carry out a series of directions.
▶ pretend to read by attending to picture clues and print when they read a trail map.
▶ demonstrate understanding of symbols by using one object to represent another.

SPOTLIGHT WORDS

binoculars • campfire • compass • environment • hike • map • mess kit • nature • tent • tracks • trail

MATERIALS

backpacks • binoculars • camping magazines • canteen • cassette tape or CD with nature sounds • clipboards • flashlights • hats • log fire pit • mess kits • old cameras • pencils • plastic compass • small sleeping bags • small tent • trail maps

PROPS

▶ **Trail Map and Pictures** (see pages 190-192 in the Appendix): Make a few copies of the trail map. If possible, enlarge the corresponding pictures.

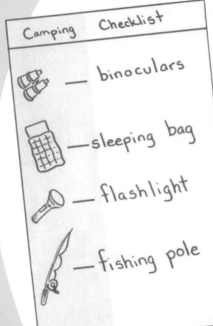

Camping Checklist

— binoculars

— sleeping bag

— flashlight

— fishing pole

▶ **Camping Checklist:** Make a checklist with items such as binoculars, backpack, shirt, pants, socks, shoes, hat, canteen, map, sleeping bag, flashlight, tent, fishing pole, and so on. Draw pictures of each item next to the word.

SETTING UP

You can make your own sleeping bags by sewing together two pieces of burlap. You can also make a fire pit by hammering together a few smooth logs into a square or triangle. (Make sure there are no rough spots that could hurt the children.) Crumple large pieces of orange and yellow paper and put them on the logs to make the fire. Play a tape or CD with nature sounds. Place all of the camping props into a large open space, such as the block area. It's also fun to take the camping props outside on the playground. Encourage the children to use trail maps to go on a hike. Place corresponding pictures on the walls, shelves, and so on for the children to find on their hike. The children can also make their own trail maps.

OPEN-ENDED QUESTIONS

What are you going to look for on your hike?
Why do animals need hiding places?
How do you think the animals feel in their hiding places?
How many different sounds can you hear?

MAKING BOOKS

▶ **A Camping We Will Go** (class book): Talk about the different things people take camping and how each item is used. Encourage the children to tell their story to their peers, emphasizing the sequence of events. Help the child write his stories on a piece of paper. Make a title page for the book ("A Camping We Will Go") and staple the pages together. As a variation, you can make a hiking book about where you would go, from start to finish, using the same process.

EXTENSION ACTIVITIES

1) Let the children create their own trail maps. Display real trail maps and their symbols to help generate ideas. Help the children understand what the different symbols on the maps mean.

2) Help the children make their own binoculars using two toilet paper rolls. Staple the two tubes together. Then, let the children decorate them with paint or markers.

3) Ask the children to bring an empty Jell-O box from home to make a camera. Cover the box with white paper and encourage the children to glue on buttons to make the control knobs. Use a clean milk lid for the lens. If desired, roll up a narrow roll of receipt paper and place inside the box for the film. Then, as the children take pictures, they roll out a small strip of paper, cut it, and draw the picture they have taken.

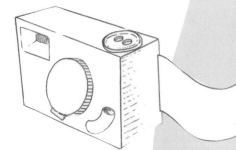

LITERACY RESOURCES— SONGS, POEMS, AND FINGERPLAYS

A Hike With My Dad (West and Cox)
My daddy is taking me on a hike.
He told me to bring some food I like.

Binoculars, water, a map in my pack.
I'm ready to carry it on my back.

The trail is windy and very steep.
And I found a feather that I'd like to keep.

A deer runs by and stops to look.
As we sit down and eat by the brook.

An eagle is soaring in the sky
I hear it screech as we walk by.

My feet are tired and I'd like to stay
But we will come back another day.

A Camping We Will Go (West and Cox)
(Tune: "The Farmer in the Dell")
A camping we will go,
A camping we will go,
Yippity, hippity, skippity, ho.
A camping we will go.

I Went Walking by Sue Williams

In the Outdoors by Kyle Carter

Just Me and My Dad by Mercer Mayer

The Listening Walk by Paul Showers

One Duck Stuck by Phyllis Root

Over in the Meadow by Ezra Jack Keats

Science

Gardener

LITERACY APPLICATION

Words Are Separated by Spaces and Made Up of Letters

Children should be given the opportunity to write independently. Supplying them with journals will give them a place to express their own thoughts and opinions. Journals help children develop a habit of writing. Children can dictate their thoughts to an adult. (It is very important to write down the child's own words.) This is a good time to point out that words are separated by spaces and made up of letters. Help children learn the difference between letters and words in sentences. When children have an understanding of this, they understand one of the concepts of reading. Encourage the children to make drawings in their journals and label them. Keep your own daily journal, too, to model the importance and enjoyment of writing. Keep in mind that journal writing should not be mandatory but done on a volunteer basis.

LITERACY OBJECTIVES

Children will:

▶ understand the relationship between spoken words and reading by asking what words say when reading labels.
▶ identify and name some letters.
▶ see print in authentic texts.
▶ learn to ask questions.

SPOTLIGHT WORDS

flower • greenhouse • grow • hoe • photosynthesis • rake • roots • shovel • soil • sprout • stem • trowel

MATERIALS

aprons • cash register • flower catalogs • flowers • garden tools • journals • markers • measuring chart • measuring sticks • money • plastic plants • Popsicle sticks with labels • pots • prizes • ribbons • sand and water table • seed packets • seeds • soil • Styrofoam pieces • vases • watering cans

PROPS

▶ **Growing Chart:** Turn a piece of paper horizontally and write "Growing Chart" at the top. Write "Name _____" and "Type of Plant _____" underneath. Divide the paper into five columns, one for each day of the week. The children can measure their plant's growth each day and record the results on their chart.

SETTING UP

Plant real seeds and flowers or use silk flowers. Put out the planting tools, pots, literature, and so on. Encourage the children to look at the seed catalogs, magazines, and packages. If planting real seeds, you may want to plant them in the sand and water table to help contain the mess. Provide markers and Popsicle sticks for the children to label plants. Encourage the children to put prices on the plants. Ask the children to guess how much their plants will grow in a certain amount of time. Use a measuring chart to record responses and information. Let the children use their journals or growing chart to record the information with text and pictures as they observe their plants grow.

OPEN-ENDED QUESTIONS

Where is the best place to plant seeds?
What seeds should you plant?
How far apart should you plant your seeds?
How much water do they need?
When is the best time to plant seeds?
What do you think your seeds will grow into?
How can you find out?

MAKING BOOKS

▶ **Seeds! Seeds!** (individual book): Before making this book, write the following poem on poster board. As you read the poem out loud, point out the spaces between the words.

*I dug a little **hole***
*And planted many **seeds**.*
*The seeds grew **sprouts**,*
*So I pulled up the **weeds**.*
*The **sun** shined brightly*
*And **sprouts** grew tall.*
*Buds became **blossoms***
*After I **watered** them all.*

Write each line on a separate piece of paper and make enough copies so that each child has all the pages. While teaching the poem, emphasize the words in boldfaced type and make word cards with corresponding pictures from the poem. Help the children see the different letters used to make up the words. Encourage the children to illustrate their books, doing only one page a day so it will not be overwhelming. See the following list for ideas:

- Hole: Glue on potting soil.
- Seeds: Use craft glue to attach real seeds.
- Sprouts: Cut out little pieces of green paper and glue to the page.
- Weeds: Collect real weeds and glue to the page.
- Sun: Draw a sun.
- Sprouts: Draw plants.
- Blossoms: Scrunch small pieces of colored tissue paper and glue to the page.
- Water: Use Q-tips and watercolor paint.
  When the children are doing their artwork, do not put your word cards at the art table because the children may try to copy your picture. This stifles their creativity. Staple all of their pages together when they finish.

EXTENSION ACTIVITIES

1) During circle time, teach the children the different names and uses of tools used in the garden.
2) Plant a seed in a clear plastic bag so the children can see the roots as it grows. Fold a wet paper towel into a little pocket and place a seed inside. Then, place the paper towel and seed into the clear plastic bag and attach it with tape to a window in your classroom. Make sure that the seed bag is at the children's eye level. Discuss how the seed will sprout and encourage the children to observe the bag each day. Make a record of the changes by taking photos or drawing pictures.

3) Let each child plant a mini garden in an egg carton. Have the children measure the different plants as they grow and record it on a chart. Discuss why different seeds grow faster than others.

LITERACY RESOURCES—SONGS, POEMS, AND FINGERPLAYS

Pumpkins (West and Cox)
Pumpkins grow from pumpkin seeds,
I planted one today.
I watered it, and pulled the weeds,
Pumpkins grow from pumpkin seeds.

Carrots…
Peppers…
Corn…
Cucumbers…

Tiny Seeds (traditional)
Tiny seed planted just right, (tuck into a ball)
Not a breath of air, not a ray of light.
Rain falls slowly to and fro',
And now the seed begins to grow. (begin to unfold)
Slowly reaching for the light,
With all its energy, all its might.
The little seed's work is almost done,
To grow up tall and face the sun. (stand up tall with arms stretched out)

LITERACY RESOURCES—BOOK LIST

Big Pumpkin by Erica Silverman
The Carrot Seed by Ruth Krauss
Growing Vegetable Soup by Lois Ehlert
It's Pumpkin Time! by Zoe Hall
Lunch by Denise Fleming
Mrs. McNosh and the Great Big Squash by Sarah Weeks
The Tiny Seed by Eric Carle
Tops and Bottoms by Janet Stevens

Space

Learning New Words and Meanings by Using Authentic Texts

Collect non-fiction and authentic books in your classroom to use as a resource to teach the children real facts in an enjoyable way. Choose books with large photographs for the children to look at. Because the text in these books may be too long to read to the children, read the text beforehand so you can summarize the information. When children are allowed to use authentic texts to gather facts and information about a subject in which they are interested, they gain an appreciation for books.

LITERACY OBJECTIVES

Children will:

▶ write their names on astronaut badges.
▶ ask questions.
▶ respond to text by providing comments.

SPOTLIGHT WORDS

craters • crew • earth • jet pack • moon • NASA • oxygen • rocket boosters • satellites • space shuttle • stars • sun

MATERIALS

astronaut helmets • jet packs • large blocks • moon and space posters • pencils • sponges for moon boots • star charts • white coats

PROPS

▶ **Astronaut Badge:** Cut out 4" circles from paper and write "Astronaut" in the middle of each one. Encourage the children to write their names on their badges and decorate them with space drawings.

▶ **Astronaut Crew List:** Write "My Astronaut Crew" at the top of a piece of lined paper. (Use the lined paper that children use to learn to practice writing.)

SETTING UP

▶ Before the children pretend to play in space, it is a good idea to give them information about what astronauts do. Use the extension activities (see page 104) to give them accurate concepts. Talk about what astronauts do and the responsibilities of each person in the crew. Then, let the children practice writing each other's names on a crew list.

1) Make jet packs by spray-painting two plastic, 2-liter soda bottles white and then taping them together with duct tape. Attach strong cord or webbing for the straps with the tape. If desired, put red and blue tape over the top of the duct tape to make stripes and put flag stickers on them for decoration.

2) Make astronaut helmets from unused fried chicken buckets. The best buckets to use are white with no writing on them. You can find these in a local grocery store that sells fried chicken. Sometimes, stores will donate them if they know how you are going to use them. Cut out an oval from one side for the children to look out of. Then have children attach flag stickers and label the helmets with their names.

3) The children will enjoy wearing "moon boots" when they pretend to walk on the moon. To make pretend moon boots, give the children thick sponges to put on the bottom of their shoes and attach them by wrapping a strong elastic band around the sponge and shoes.

4) Put all of the space props in a large area. Have markers or colored pencils for the children to write their names on their astronaut badges. Hang up posters of the moon, earth, and space on the walls.

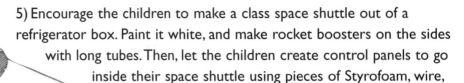

5) Encourage the children to make a class space shuttle out of a refrigerator box. Paint it white, and make rocket boosters on the sides with long tubes. Then, let the children create control panels to go inside their space shuttle using pieces of Styrofoam, wire, pipe cleaners, paper plates, and cups. The children could also use blocks or large pieces of Styrofoam to make a space shuttle.

OPEN-ENDED QUESTIONS

What can you tell me about your space shuttle?
Where are you going?
How many places will you go?
What does an astronaut do?
How long will you be in space?

MAKING BOOKS

▶ **Off With an Alien** (class or individual book): Make books for each child by cutting out the spaceship pattern for the pages of the book (see page 203 in the Appendix). Then, put out authentic nonfiction books for the children. Encourage the children to create a story about an alien from outer space learning factual information about space. (Make sure the children know that aliens are not real.) The children can choose facts learned previously in class or use information found in the authentic texts when writing their stories. Help the children use new words they have learned. Then let the children illustrate their text, cut out the alien patterns, and attach them with string to the title page. Then, the alien can float around in space. Staple all of the pages together to complete their books.

EXTENSION ACTIVITIES

1) Check out a book about space from your local library. Show the children selected parts about things you have been discussing in class. Talking about space can be very abstract for young children, so it is good for them to see what space is really like by looking at books about real astronauts in space.

2) Teach the children about the moon and the sun. Provide books with large, clear photographs. It is best to stay close to subjects that the children can associate with when they are young.

3) Let the children make their own space shuttles by attaching cardboard triangle wings to a toilet paper roll and then painting it white. Let it dry and then decorate it with markers. Hang up a real photograph of a space shuttle for the children to see while they put the details on their space shuttle. Then stretch out cording between two objects, thread the

space shuttle on the string, and let the children push it to see how far it will go. The children can have races to see whose shuttle is fastest.

LITERACY RESOURCES— SONGS, POEMS, AND FINGERPLAYS

Blast Off (West and Cox)
Ten, nine, eight—we can't be late. (loud)
Up in the sky, we will fly. (soft)
Seven, six, five—happy to be alive. (loud)
Off to a star that's very far. (soft)

Four, three, two—just me and you. (loud)
A stop at the moon just before noon. (soft)

One at last—off we blast. (loud)

10, 9, 8, 7, 6, 5, 4, 3, 2, 1 - BLAST OFF! (soft to loud)

Zoom, Zoom, Zoom (traditional)
Zoom, zoom, zoom, (stand, rub hands upwards)
I'm going to the moon. (zoom hands up)
If you want to take a trip,
Climb aboard my rocket ship. (climb imaginary ladder)
Zoom, zoom, zoom, (repeat hand-rubbing)
I'm going to the moon.

LITERACY RESOURCES—BOOK LIST

I Want to Be an Astronaut by Byron Barton
The Moon by Seymour Simon
Mooncake by Frank Asch
Papa, Please Get the Moon for Me by Eric Carle
The Space Shuttle by Jacqueline Langille and Bobbie Kalman
The Sun by Seymour Simon
Zoom! Zoom! Zoom! I'm Off to the Moon by Dan Yaccarino

Chemist

LITERACY APPLICATION

Sharing Information

Children should engage in informal conversations daily, so encourage conversation by asking open-ended questions such as "Why?" "How?" and "What if…?". Oral language and problem-solving skills will increase as the children formulate thoughts through inquiry. As the children pretend to be chemists, they learn to communicate with their peers about their findings.

LITERACY OBJECTIVES

Children will:

▶ practice writing when making observations.

▶ understand that symbols have meaning while reading charts.

▶ ask questions.

SPOTLIGHT WORDS

attract • chemicals • chemist • evaluation • experiment • float • lab • mix • observations • prediction • pressure • repel • scientist • sink • solution

MATERIALS

clipboards • eyedroppers • gloves • magnifying glasses • measuring cups • microscope • pencils • plastic beakers • plastic test tubes • prediction charts • test tube holders • white coats

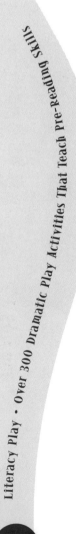

PROPS

- **Report Form:** Write the following lines on a piece of paper, leaving space between each one for the children to write their thoughts.

  Dr. _____, the Scientist (write this at the top of the page)

  My Science Experiment:

  These are the things I need:

  _____

  _____

  I think this mixture could be used:

  Make enough copies so that each child has one.

SETTING UP

Set up your dramatic play area to look like a science lab. Decide what kind of scientific problem the children will attempt to solve. Set out the appropriate science props and encourage the children to come up with solutions. Bring the sand and water table over to the science lab and let the children experiment with baking soda and vinegar, mix colored water in test tubes, make oobleck, or melt ice blocks with salt water. Encourage the children to write about their experiments on their report form. Attach their report form to a clipboard for fun.

OPEN-ENDED QUESTIONS

What do you think will happen next?

What would you do differently next time?

Why do you think that happened?

What is different?

What is the same?

MAKING BOOKS

- **Snap, Fizzle, Pop** (class book): Turn a piece of paper horizontally and write "Prediction Chart" at the top. On the top half of the paper, write "What do you think will happen?" Leave enough space for the child to write a response (and illustrate it). On the second half, write, "What happened?" The children can use this space to record what happened. Make a copy for each child in the class. Then, do an experiment with the children. Before you do the experiment, ask the children what they think will happen and record their responses on their pages. Encourage the children to illustrate their responses. After the experiment, have the children dictate what happened as you write it on their pages. Put all of the pages together to make a book.

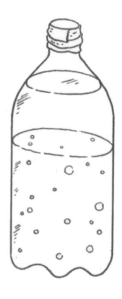

EXTENSION ACTIVITIES

1) Invite a chemist to come in and conduct chemical experiments.

2) Make science bottles using plastic soda bottles. Pour oil and colored water into the bottle and glue on the lid. For variety add glitter, confetti, crayon shavings, and other objects in the oil and water. Encourage the children to tip the bottle to observe what happens.

3) To find many science experiments appropriate for young children, look at the Science section of *Sand and Water Play* (West and Cox, Gryphon House, 2001).

LITERACY RESOURCES—SONGS, POEMS, AND FINGERPLAYS

Experiments (West and Cox)
Mix, measure, stir,
Think and observe.
Look for details,
No one ever fails.
Record every guess,
Make up tests.
Stretch your mind,
And you will find
Experiment is done.
Science is fun!

Fizzle, Snap, Pop (West and Cox)
Fizzle, snap, pop,
That's how the mixture goes.
Fizzle, snap, pop,
Stand back in case it blows.

LITERACY RESOURCES—BOOK LIST

Inch by Inch by Leo Lionni
What Is a Scientist? by Barbara Lehn
What Magnets Can Do by Allan Fowler

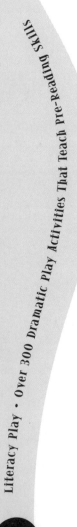

Rock Hound

LITERACY APPLICATION

Letter-Like Forms and Letters

Children use marks and real letters to represent sound values and meaning. These marks or letters put together sporadically represent their thoughts. After children have written a series of letter-like forms or letters, they often ask what they represent. They feel excited and proud about what they have written. For example, they may say, "What did I write?" or "What does this say?" This shows that children attach meaning to what they are writing—they understand the concept that marks, scribbles, and letters have meaning. When you read what the children have written phonetically, they are often surprised because it did not say what they intended. This helps children move to the next stage, which is an understanding that letters must be put into a correct sequence. Then they will ask, "How do you spell _____?" Allow children to go through these stages at their own pace. When children look for rocks and make labels for the rock displays, they are writing marks and letters to represent their ideas.

LITERACY OBJECTIVES

Children will:

‣ pretend to read labels by attending to pictures.
‣ attempt writing using alphabet letters when making signs.

hE LIKrErr ....ʋɯˈᵗʳɯ⌣⌣

SPOTLIGHT WORDS

big • crystals • heavy • large • light • little • medium • rough • sharp • small • smooth

MATERIALS

books • crystals • magnifying glasses • paper labels • rock chart • rock collection bags • rock samples

SETTING UP

Set up your dramatic play area to look like a rock shop or museum with long display tables. Ask the children to help you set out the rocks for display. Take the children on a walk outdoors to find different kinds of rocks. Give the children clipboards and pencils to write the description of the rocks they find. Hang up charts and pictures of rocks for the children to look at. Help the children decide what kind of rock it is by looking at the chart and books. Then, let the children label their rocks and displays.

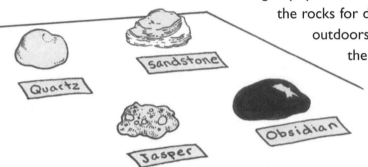

OPEN-ENDED QUESTIONS

What does your rock feel like?
What does your rock look like?

MAKING BOOKS

▶ **My Pet Rock** (individual book): Divide a sheet of plain paper into four squares. In the middle of one square, write: "My Pet Rock" by _____. Write the following sentences on the bottom of the squares, one sentence per square.

My pet rock's name is _____.
My pet rock likes to _____.
My pet rock has _____.

Make copies for each child in the class and cut out the squares. The children can fill in the blanks and illustrate the pages. Staple the pages together to make a book. If desired, make more pages for the book using your own sentences.

EXTENSION ACTIVITIES

1) Make fossils out of plaster of Paris or playdough.
2) Help the children grow crystals (see the recipe on the following page). You can make different kinds such as salt, sugar, alum, and ammonia crystal and compare their size and shape.

Crystals Recipe

1 ½ cups water

3 cups sugar or salt

Bring water to a boil and add sugar or salt, one spoonful at a time, stirring so that the sugar completely dissolves. Continue adding sugar until it is a clear syrup, then pour it into three clear jars. Add food coloring to the syrup or leave it clear. Tie a string to a pencil and attach a weight (paper clip) on the end of the string. Put the string into the syrup. It takes about a week for crystals to form on the string. Carefully break the crust that forms on the top of the syrup every day to allow the syrup to evaporate. Be careful not to disturb it while the crystals are forming.

3) Encourage the children to find a stone, and then let them paint it to make a paperweight. Help them write their names on it, too.

LITERACY RESOURCES—SONGS, POEMS, AND FINGERPLAYS

Rocks, Rocks, Everywhere (West and Cox)

Rocks are here,
Rocks are there,
Rocks are everywhere.

Shiny rocks, jagged rocks,
Pretty rocks too.
Put them in your pocket
For me and for you.

A Geologist (West and Cox)

A geologist I hope to be,
I'll examine all the rocks I see.
I'll dig here, and chisel there.
I'll search for rocks everywhere.

LITERACY RESOURCES—BOOK LIST

If You Find a Rock by Peggy Christian
Let's Go Rock Collecting by Roma Gans
Rock Collecting by Roma Gans
Rocks in His Head by Carol Otis Hurst

Stores

Pizza Parlor
Loving Books Motivates Reading

Shoe Store
Taking Turns in Conversation

Restaurant
Picture Clues

Ice Cream Parlor
Syllable Blending and Segmenting

Grocery Store
Environmental Print

Pet Shop
Writing Letter-Like Forms and Letters

Pizza Parlor

LITERACY APPLICATION

Loving Books Motivates Reading

Children enjoy reading and writing when it is amusing and fun. Books such as *Silly Sally* by Audrey Wood or *The Napping House* by Don and Audrey Wood help children gain a love of words and books. By creating silly stories, children have an opportunity to be silly in appropriate ways. When their interest is high and they are having fun, they are motivated to read and write.

LITERACY OBJECTIVES

Children will:

▶ identify some letters from menus and ingredient lists.

▶ improve their listening skills by following directions.

▶ write using letter-like forms when taking orders and making signs.

SPOTLIGHT WORDS

cold • delivery • dough • ingredients • hot • order • oven

MATERIALS

aprons • cash register • empty pizza boxes • menus • money • "Open" and "Closed" signs • order forms • pencils • plastic dishes • plastic pizza • plastic pizza cutter • tablecloth • telephones

PROPS

▶ **Ordering Pads** (see page 194 in the Appendix): Make a few copies of this page, cut out guest checks, and staple them together to make order pads.

▶ **Toppings List:** On a chart, write a list of different pizza toppings. Illustrate each item.

Toppings List

 pepperoni

 mushrooms

 anchovies

 banana peppers

Literacy Play • Over 300 Dramatic Play Activities That Teach Pre-Reading Skills

SETTING UP

Put pizza parlor props in the dramatic play area. You may want to add playdough so the children can make playdough pizzas. Encourage the children to use ordering pads to take orders. Display the toppings chart and discuss the different toppings a pizza can have. Help the children make "Open" and "Closed" signs for their parlor.

OPEN-ENDED QUESTIONS

Have you ever been to a pizza parlor?
What kind of things can you put on a pizza?

MAKING BOOKS

▶ **Our Pizza Book** (class or individual book): Put out collage materials and glue to make pizzas. Materials could include:

> Cheese: shredded yellow construction paper
> Peppers: small green construction paper triangles
> Black olives: small O-shaped circles cut from black
>   construction paper
> Pepperoni: red or brown construction paper circles
> Tomato sauce: one large red construction paper circle
> Dough: one tan construction paper circle, larger than red circle

Let the children use the collage materials to make a pizza on their paper. Encourage them to be creative and come up with their own toppings. Ask each child what kind of pizza he likes and record his response underneath his pizza if he cannot write it himself.

▶ **Silly Pizza Book** (class book): Create a classroom "silly pizza" book. Use a paper-plate pizza (see #4 in Extension Activities) as the cover and cut out circles of paper for the inside pages. Staple them together. Help the children get started by asking them an open-ended question such as, "What would happen if you had to eat a pizza as big as your house?" or "What would happen if you put a pizza on your Grandma's rocking chair?" or "What if a dinosaur came to your pizza party?" Record the children's responses and let them illustrate it when finished.

EXTENSION ACTIVITIES

1) Have a pizza delivered to your classroom and talk about all the different things that have to happen before it gets there, such as writing down the order, making the pizza, and delivering it.

2) Help the children make their own individual pizzas. Use refrigerated biscuit dough for the crust. Let the children roll out the dough and choose different kinds of toppings for their pizzas.

3) Go on a field trip to a pizza parlor. Focus on all the different steps involved in making a pizza.

4) Encourage the children to make paper-plate pizzas in the art area to use as thank-you notes to send to the pizza parlor they visit. Children can use paper plates for the crust, red colored glue for the sauce, and yellow yarn for the cheese. They can decorate their pizza as desired, such as cutting out little construction paper circles for pepperoni. Help them write thank-you messages on the backs of the plates.

LITERACY RESOURCES— SONGS, POEMS, AND FINGERPLAYS

Pizza (West and Cox)
(Tune: "Row, Row, Row Your Boat")
Munch, munch, munch your pizza
Eat it while it's hot.
Melted cheese and pepperoni,
I sure want a lot.

Ham, olives, green peppers,
Canadian bacon too.
Pineapple and sausage,
You can make it, too.

Make a Pizza*
Make a pizza pat, pat, pat. (pat hands together)
Do not make it fat, fat, fat. (stretch hands apart)
You must make it flat, flat, flat. (pat hands together)
Make a pizza just like that. (clap hands together)
* Adapted from "Make a Pancake"

LITERACY RESOURCES—BOOK LIST

The Little Red Hen (Makes a Pizza) by Philemon Sturges
Pete's a Pizza by William Steig
Pizza for Sam by Mary Labatt
Pizza Pat by Will Terry
The Pizza That We Made by Joan Holub
Sam's Pizza: Your Pizza to Go by David Pelham

Shoe Store

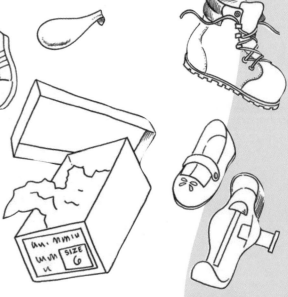

LITERACY APPLICATION

Taking Turns in Conversations

In a dramatic play setting, conversations are more likely to be open and non-threatening. Join the children's play in the shoe store, but be careful not to dominate their conversation. Children should take the lead in conversations when teachers enter their play. Respond briefly and make comments that encourage the children to talk more. Be sure to model listening. When children are conversing back and forth with their peers, it is important to stand back and listen as they exchange ideas and thoughts. Through conversations, children learn how to use language to express their ideas.

LITERACY OBJECTIVES

Children will:

▶ recognize and name some letters on signs and boxes.

SPOTLIGHT WORDS

big • length • measure • medium • size • small • width

MATERIALS

cardstock • cash register • colored pencils • crayons • different colors of paper • empty shoe polish containers • foot measure • grocery bags • markers • money • price tags • shoe horn • shoeboxes • shoelaces • shoes

PROPS

▶ **Shoe Size Chart:** Write "Shoe Size" and "Color Chart" at the top of the paper (horizontal). Record the number of the same size and color of shoes on the chart.

▶ **Shoe Tying Pattern** (see page 195 in the Appendix): Make copies of the shoe pattern (one pair for each child in the class), glue the pages onto cardstock, and cut out the shoes. Punch holes for the shoelaces and thread them through. Give a pair to each child and show them how to tie a shoe.

SETTING UP

Set up a large area to look like a shoe store. Display different shoes and boxes. Encourage the children to classify the shoes into different categories, such as by occupation, use, size, color, and tread. Let the children put different prices on the shoes using sticky notes or different colored paper for price tags. Have a measuring device for sizing shoes, so the children can see what size their feet are.

OPEN-ENDED QUESTIONS

Which one is longer?
How are these shoes alike?
Why do you think they are different?

MAKING BOOKS

▶ **Lots of Shoes** (class or individual book): Show the children many different kinds of shoes, such as running shoes, water shoes, cowboy boots, hiking boots, ballet shoes, and so on. Encourage the children to take turns talking about who wears these different kinds of shoes. Give each child a shoe pattern (see page 195 in the Appendix). Encourage the children to decorate it to look like the kind of shoe they would like to wear. Record on each child's page what type of shoe it is and why he wants to wear it. Staple the pages together to make a book.

EXTENSION ACTIVITIES

1) Teach the children about different shoes that people wear for different jobs and in different cultures. Encourage the children to make a book about different shoes and when they are used.

2) Make a chart of the color and size of the children's shoes in your classroom.

3) Make playdough prints with shoe treads. Let the children compare the different treads.

LITERACY RESOURCES— SONGS, POEMS, AND FINGERPLAYS

New Shoes (West and Cox)
Come quick and see
What I have new.
Mom just bought me
Shoes that are blue.

They help me jump
They help me run.
I am having
So much fun!

Cobbler, Cobbler (traditional)
Cobbler, cobbler, mend my shoe.
Get it doe by half past two.
My little toe is peeping through.
Cobbler, cobbler, mend my shoe.
Get it done by half past two.

LITERACY RESOURCES—BOOK LIST

The Foot Book by Dr. Suess
New Shoes for Silvia by Johanna Hurwitz
A Pair of Red Sneakers by Lisa Lawston
Shoes by Elizabeth Winthrop
Whose Shoes? by Margaret Miller

Restaurant

LITERACY APPLICATION

Picture Clues

Connecting a word with a picture is an important concept for children to learn. Menus are a great way for children to see a picture and word together, which allows them to pretend to read and feel like a reader. When children can visualize the word with a picture, it helps them to remember it. They begin to associate the meaning of the word with the picture and gain an understanding that print is different than pictures. As children learn to read, attending to picture clues tells them what the print on a page represents. Formulating ideas from pictures is a reading skill.

LITERACY OBJECTIVES

Children will:

▶ write using letter-like forms when writing on order pads and signs.
▶ pretend to read by attending to picture clues on menus.
▶ respond appropriately in conversations and to questions.

SPOTLIGHT WORDS

chef • culture • ethnic • manners • menu • napkins • order • utensils • waiter • waitress

MATERIALS

aprons • cash register • chef hats • chop sticks (if appropriate) • flower in a vase • menus (different ethnic foods) • money • napkins • order pads • pictures of different cultures • plastic utensils • play dishes • play foods • tubs

PROPS

▶ **Order Pads** (see page 194 in the Appendix): Make a few copies of this page, cut out guest checks, and staple them together to make order pads.

▶ **Menu With Pictures:** Make your own menus by writing the names and prices of different foods and illustrating each one.

SETTING UP

Set up the dramatic play area to look like a restaurant. Use more than one table, if possible. Put out order pads and menus. Make sure that the menus have items with corresponding pictures and point out the different words and pictures. Help the children make "Open" and "Closed" signs. Encourage the children to take on different roles such as the chef, waitress, waiter, bus person, patron, and hostess.

OPEN-ENDED QUESTIONS

What things can you smell?
What do you want to order?
What kinds of food are you cooking?

MAKING BOOKS

▶ **My Favorite Food Is...** (class book): At the top of a piece of white paper write, "Open a menu and what do I see?" At the bottom write, "I see a _____ just for me." Make a copy for each child in the class. Ask the children to write or dictate their favorite food and put it in the blank. Bring in different ads, labels, magazines, logos, and so on for the children to use to cut out their favorite food and glue on their page. Staple the pages together to make a book. As the children read the book, they will be able to look at the picture and guess the text.

EXTENSION ACTIVITIES

1) Show the children menus from different ethnic restaurants. Talk about different cultures and the foods that people eat.
2) Go on a field trip to a restaurant. Ask the children to pay attention to when the waiter or waitress listens to customers and writes down orders.
3) Put different foods into separate plastic cups. Cover the cups with aluminum foil, punch a few holes in the top of each, and let the children smell each one. Ask them to guess what is in the cups using their sense of smell.

LITERACY RESOURCES—
SONGS, POEMS, AND FINGERPLAYS

Restaurant (West and Cox)
(Tune: "The Wheels on the Bus")
The chef in the kitchen goes chop, chop, chop.
Chop, chop, chop. Chop, chop, chop.
The chef in the kitchen goes chop, chop, chop,
Fixing food for you.

The chef in the kitchen goes stir, stir, stir...
The chef in the kitchen goes spread, spread, spread...
The chef in the kitchen goes fry, fry, fry...
The chef in the kitchen goes bake, bake, bake...

Yummy (West and Cox)
My nose tells my tummy
It's going to be yummy.
I look at the menu
And eat bread and honey.

I sit still in my seat
Because soon we will eat.
The food was delicious.
Mom, may I have a treat?

LITERACY RESOURCES—BOOK LIST

Bread, Bread, Bread by Ann Morris
Pass the Fritters, Critters by Cheryl Chapman
Rice by Pam Robson
Rice Is Life by Rita Golden Gelman

Ice Cream Parlor

LITERACY APPLICATION

Syllable Blending and Segmenting

Syllable clapping builds phonological awareness in preschoolers by drawing attention to the sounds of speech. Clapping out the syllables breaks down the words into smaller components, which helps the children hear the different parts of a word. Children can clap out the syllables of the ice cream flavors in the ice cream parlor.

LITERACY OBJECTIVES

Children will:

▶ identify and match words from the flavor list.
▶ write using alphabet-like letters while writing orders and names on tokens.
▶ use critical listening skills by discussing personal preferences or dislikes.
▶ clap out syllables of ice cream flavors.

SPOTLIGHT WORDS

cream • dairy • flavor • freeze • melt • milk • mix • scoop

MATERIALS

bowls • cardboard or plastic cones • cash register • colored plastic balls or playdough (for ice cream) • empty ice cream cartons and buckets • ice cream scoops • menu • money • plastic banana split dishes • spoons • tokens

Ice Cream Chart		
Chocolate	Strawberry	Vanilla
Jared	Jamie	Candice
Garrett	Courtney	Allison
Kimberly	Brooke	Fallon
Phillip		Devon

PROPS

▶ **Ice Cream Chart:** Make a three-column chart. Label the first column "Chocolate," the second column "Strawberry," and the third column "Vanilla." Take a poll and write down the children's favorite ice cream flavor.

SETTING UP

Set up the ice cream parlor with tables and props. You can use the sand and water table as a counter. Use plastic colored balls or playdough for the pretend ice cream. If desired, use carts to take the ice cream around to the children. Help the children make a flavor list and labels for their ice cream and write prices on a price board. Ask the children to write a child's name on a token and then pass them out. Teach the children "Yippety, Splickety" (on the next page) and talk about syllables in the ice cream flavors.

OPEN-ENDED QUESTIONS

What's your favorite kind of ice cream?
How do you make ice cream?

MAKING BOOKS

▶ **Ice Cream Book** (class book): Make copies of the ice cream cone pattern (see page 206 in the Appendix), one for each child. Cut out ice cream cones and give one to each child. Ask the children to write their favorite type of ice cream on the scoop and then color it. As they tell you what their ice cream flavor is, help them to clap out the syllables. Let the children come up with the title of their book and write it on a blank scoop. Staple all the pages together. After completing the book, read it together as a group and encourage the children to clap out the syllables.

EXTENSION ACTIVITIES

1) Let the children help you make ice cream. Talk about where ice cream comes from and how it is made. You can make individual portions and flavors in a can. Get two different sizes of tin or plastic cans with lids. Put ice and rock salt in the bigger can and in the smaller can, put cream, flavoring, sugar, milk, and eggs. Then, place the lid on the smaller can and put it inside the bigger can. Put the lid on the bigger can and roll it back and forth until you have made ice cream.

ice & rock salt

cream flavoring

← put the lid on tight!

LITERACY RESOURCES—
SONGS, POEMS, AND FINGERPLAYS

Ice Cream (traditional)
You scream, I scream,
We all scream for ice cream.

Yippety, Splickety (West and Cox)
Yippety, splickety, lick ice cream,
There is a flavor that makes me scream.
Chocolate! (shout)
Chocolate. (whisper)
Cho-co-late. (clap syllables)
(Other flavors to use: straw-ber-ry, va-ni-lla, o-range, and so on)

LITERACY RESOURCES—BOOK LIST

From Cow to Ice Cream by Bertram T. Knight
Ice Cream Larry by Jill Pinkwater and Daniel Manus Pinkwater
I Like Ice Cream by Robin Pickering
Isaac the Ice Cream Truck by Scott Santoro
Milk to Ice Cream by Inez Snyder

Grocery Store

LITERACY APPLICATION

Environmental Print

The term "environmental print" refers to letters or words that children see in the world around them, such as billboards, signs, labels, bumper stickers, cereal boxes, gum wrappers, fast food restaurant logos, banners, and so on. Print that children see frequently becomes familiar to them, and they feel confident when reading it. Hiebert and Ham (1981) documented that "children who were taught to read and write with environmental print learned significantly more letter names and sounds than did children who learned alphabet letters without using environmental print." The grocery store is the perfect place for children to see environmental print.

LITERACY OBJECTIVES

Children will:
▶ read environmental print on labels.
▶ identify and name some letters.
▶ match words and letters when using food labels and coupons.
▶ write using letter-like forms by making shopping lists and writing checks.
▶ understand that letters become words.

SPOTLIGHT WORDS

bakery • coupon • deli • food groups (meat, dairy, vegetables and fruits, grains) • grocer • lists • nutrition • prices • produce

MATERIALS

cash registers • checkbooks • coupons • empty grocery containers • grocery ads • old credit cards • paper sacks • paper for grocery lists • play money • purses • small grocery carts and baskets • wallets

PROPS

▸ **Checks** (see page 196 in the Appendix).

▸ **Credit Card** (see page 196 in the Appendix).

▸ **Grocery List:** Write "Grocery List" on the top of a long sheet of paper. Make enough copies so that the children can have at least one. The children can use these to write down groceries they want to buy.

▸ **Sale/Special Signs:** Write "Sale" at the top of a piece of poster board or chart paper, and write "Special" at the top of another piece. Make a few of these. The children can use them to write down sale items.

SETTING UP

Put the grocery props in a large area, such as the block area. If desired, let the children classify the groceries into sections such as dairy, meat, produce, and so on. Then, help the children make labels for these sections. Encourage the children to look at the grocery ads and then make a list of what groceries they want to buy. Let the children match the grocery products with their coupons. Encourage the children to practice writing their names on pretend checks or credit cards.

OPEN-ENDED QUESTIONS

What are you going to buy?
What could you put on your shopping list?

MAKING BOOKS

▸ **Groceries** (class book): Fill a three-ring binder with 26 clear cover sheets. Write the letters of the alphabet on separate pieces of paper and put each one inside a cover sheet. Ask each child to bring in a label from cans, boxes, ads, magazines, and other environmental print from home. Encourage the children to search through the letters in the binder to find the corresponding letter on their label. Let the children glue their label on the appropriate page. Add more pages as needed to the binder. This is a book the children can add to over a long period of time.

▸ **In My Cart** (individual book): Give the children grocery ads and magazines and encourage them to cut out pictures of environmental print. Ask the children to glue their pictures on strips of cardstock, and then help them write the names of the items underneath. Help the children staple their pages together to make a book in the shape of a shopping cart.

EXTENSION ACTIVITIES

1) Talk about the importance of proper nutrition and healthy eating habits. Introduce the food pyramid and ask the children to classify the foods into the correct groups.

2) Go to a grocery store in your neighborhood. Divide the children into groups (with an adult in each group) and ask each group to go to a different department. Give the children clipboards to draw pictures of what they see. When you come back to class, have each group report to the rest of the children about what they saw.

3) Encourage the children to make their own coupons.

4) Choose a simple recipe to make. Make a grocery list with the children, go and buy the groceries at the grocery store, and then help the children prepare and cook the food.

5) Ask the children to collect labels from home and bring them in. Help the children group the labels according to their first letter and then display them on posters or bulletin boards.

LITERACY RESOURCES— SONGS, POEMS, AND FINGERPLAYS

To Market (West and Cox)

To market, to market
To buy a dozen eggs.
Home again, home again,
Run with my legs.

To market, to market
To buy some bread.
Home again, home again,
I will be fed.

To market, to market
To buy milk in a jug.
Home again, home again,
I'll fill up my mug.

To market, to market
To buy a some meat.
Home again, home again,
To cook something to eat.

To market, to market
To buy bananas in a bunch.
Home again, home again,
Time for lunch.

To market, to market
To buy veggies by the heap.
Home again, home again,
I'm going to sleep.

LITERACY RESOURCES—BOOK LIST

Eating the Alphabet by Lois Ehlert
The Edible Pyramid: Good Eating Every Day by Loreen Leedy
Gregory, the Terrible Eater by Mitchell Sharmat
Just Enough Carrots by Stuart J. Murphy
Lunch by Denise Fleming

Pet Shop

LITERACY APPLICATION

Writing Letter-Like Forms and Letters

Provide children with opportunities to write through play. Giving children a variety of props such as different shapes and colors of paper and different writing tools will help trigger their interest. When children write during dramatic play, they are exploring and discovering at their own pace. Literacy props in the pet shop encourage children to continue exploring without threatening those children who may not be ready. It is important to accept all levels of writing in the classroom, including letter-like forms as well as letters. When children are ready to write, the opportunity will be there.

LITERACY OBJECTIVES

Children will:

▶ pretend to read print and see that print is meaningful by reading pet information and labels.

▶ write using letter-like forms when writing the names of their pets and making signs.

SPOTLIGHT WORDS

big • breed • fur • groom • hard • little • long • paws • short • soft

MATERIALS

cash register • coupons • leashes • pet care notes • pet collar with ID tag • pet dishes • pet toys (squeaky toys, soft balls, and so on) • play money • shopping baskets • signs • stuffed animals

PROPS

▶ Pet Care Notes: Cut paper in half. Write "My Pet" at the top of each half. Then fill in the rest of the paper with the following details, leaving a space after each line:

Name of Pet:
Kind of Pet:
Special Care:

SETTING UP

Set up the dramatic play area to look like a pet store. Let the children arrange and classify the different stuffed animals. Put out other pet care items to buy and sell. Let the children make Open and Closed signs, ID tags, and pet care instructions for the animals. Then, let the children pretend to read pet care information to the customers when they buy a pet (stuffed animal).

OPEN-ENDED QUESTIONS

Does your pet need love?
How do you show your love?
How do pets need to be touched?
Are all pets handled in the same way?
What kind of home does your pet need?
Why does it need food?
What is its tail for?

MAKING BOOKS

▶ **Our Pets** (class book): Write the following sentence on the top of a piece of paper: "Whose Favorite Pet is a _____?" Make enough copies so that each child gets one. Encourage the children to draw their pet and write its name on the page using letter-like forms and letters. (If the child doesn't have a pet, he can draw any pet that he knows.) Cut strips of paper 6" x 3", give one to each child, and help him write his name on one side. Take a picture of each child, cut it out, and glue it on the bottom of the page. Staple the strip of paper on top of the child's picture so the child's name and picture are not showing. Make a title page, "Our Pets," and staple all of the pages together to make a book. The children can look at the picture of the pet, guess whose it is, and flip over the strip of paper to see the child's picture and name. This book is a fun game as well as a book.

EXTENSION ACTIVITIES

1) Get a class pet and let the children help take care of it.

2) Invite a groomer to come in and demonstrate how to groom an animal.

3) Take a survey of what everyone's favorite animal is and make a chart with the results.

LITERACY RESOURCES—
SONGS, POEMS, AND FINGERPLAYS

How Much Is That Pet in the Window?* (Tune: "How Much Is That Doggie in the Window?")

How much is that kitty in the window?
The one with the spot on her ear.
How much is that kitty in the window?
She'll surely be my little dear.

How much is that fishy in the fish bowl?
The one swimming up and down.
How much is that fishy in the fish bowl?
I'll show it to my friend in town.

How much is that gecko in the cage?
The one looking just right at me.
How much is that gecko in the cage?
I wonder how much he will be.

How much is that slithering snake?
The long one curled up in the box.
How much is that slithering snake?
My sister will sure get a shock.

How much is that funny little turtle?
The one with the shell green and blue.
How much is that funny little turtle?
I'll bring him home for me and you.
* Adapted from traditional

Little Green Turtle (West and Cox)

Little green turtle go slow, very slow.
See how his shell drags low, very low.

See how his head moves in and out.
When the children scream, run, and shout.

See how his feet go pitter, patter, pitter.
Don't you think he's a cute little critter?

LITERACY RESOURCES—BOOK LIST

Clifford, the Small Red Puppy by Norman Bridwell
Moonbear's Pet by Frank Asch
Whistle for Willie by Ezra Jack Keats

Transportation

Traffic
Print Has Practical Uses

Airplane
Capitalization: Upper- and Lowercase Letters

Train
Alliteration: Sounds of Letters

Travel
Sharing Books

Traffic

LITERACY APPLICATION

Print Has Practical Uses

At an early age children notice signs on the street. Adults can help children recognize the importance of the words on these signs. By pointing out individual letters and words on traffic signs, children will see that signs give directions and information. This is an easy and convenient way to increase literacy skills. Reading signs develops the children's knowledge and vocabulary to help them become successful readers. As children create their own traffic signs and use them as they play, they see that print has practical uses.

LITERACY OBJECTIVES

Children will:

▶ understand the function of print by reading traffic signs.
▶ demonstrate good listening skills by carrying out a series of directions.

SPOTLIGHT WORDS

crosswalk • intersection • laws • pedestrians • railroad crossing • rules • seatbelts • stop sign • traffic light • yield

MATERIALS

bikes • paper • pencils

PROPS

▶ **License Plate:** Cut pieces of poster board the same size as license plates. The children can choose states and decorate as desired.
▶ **Traffic Signs:** Make a few traffic signs, such as caution, stop, pedestrian crossing, and yield. Have a few blank signs for the children to create their own.
▶ **Driver's License:** Make driver's licenses by cutting paper or cardstock into small rectangles and writing "Driver's License" at the top. On the left-hand side, write "Name," "Age," and "Birthday." Then draw a small oval shape on the right side for the children to draw a picture of their face. Make enough copies so that each child has one.

SETTING UP

Help the children create traffic signs and put them outside in the playground area. Put up the traffic signs you have made, too. Have paper license plates for the children to write their names on and decorate. Tape the license plate on the bike. Help the children create names to put on street signs. Then, encourage the children to follow the signs while riding their bikes.

OPEN-ENDED QUESTIONS

Why do we need to follow traffic signs?
What does this sign mean?

MAKING BOOKS

Transportation Vehicles (individual book): Using the transportation patterns (see pages 207-210 in the Appendix), make quite a few copies of each page. Then, cut out different shapes to make traffic sign pages, such as an octagon for a stop sign, a rectangle for a speed limit sign, a triangle for a yield sign, and a circle for a railroad crossing sign. Let the children choose which shapes they want to use in their book. For example, they could have two blank car pages and then an octagon page, three more blank car pages and then a rectangle page. Help the children write the words "stop," "yield," and "speed limit," on their sign pages. Encourage the children to create their own progressive stories with title pages and illustrations. Let the children write as much as they can independently. As the children incorporate the traffic signs into their stories, they will see the practical use of print.

EXTENSION ACTIVITIES

1) Give the children clipboards and then take them outside to a parking lot. Ask them to look at the cars and classify them into groups. Then have the children tally the cars and share their results.
2) Help the children make cars out of boxes. Cut a hole in the bottom of the box that is big enough for the child to fit through (adult only). Turn the box upside down and attach suspenders to the box (to go over the child's shoulders). Then, let the children paint and decorate their boxes to look like cars. Have paper license plates for the children to write on and then glue to their cars.
3) Teach the children what different traffic signs mean. Talk about car safety with the children. Discuss how important it is to wear seatbelts and cross the road safely.

Transportation

LITERACY RESOURCES—
SONGS, POEMS, AND FINGERPLAYS

Stop, Look, and Listen (traditional)

Stop, look, and listen
Before you cross the street.
First use your eyes and ears,
Then use your feet.

The Wheels on the Bus (traditional)

The wheels on the bus go 'round and 'round.
'Round and 'round, 'round and 'round.
The wheels on the bus go 'round and 'round,
All around the town.

The windshield wipers go swish, swish, swish…
The baby on the bus goes, "Wah, wah, wah"…
People on the bus go up and down…
The horn on the bus goes beep, beep, beep…
The money on the bus goes clink, clink, clink…
The driver on the bus says, "Move on back"…

LITERACY RESOURCES—BOOK LIST

Truck by Donald Crews
The Wheels on the Bus by Penny Dann
The Wheels on the Bus by Raffi

Airplane

LITERACY APPLICATION

Capitalization: Upper- and Lowercase Letters

After children understand the meaning and purpose of letters, they can begin to distinguish between upper- and lowercase letters. Children often learn uppercase letters first because they are easier to write. It is also easier for children to identify uppercase letters because their own names are capitalized. When reading text, though, most letters are lowercase. It is important for children to learn that although upper- and lowercase letters look different, they mean the same thing. Children will be able to practice matching upper- and lowercase letters when finding seats in the airplane. This will help them when they need to understand capitalization.

LITERACY OBJECTIVES

Children will:
- recognize and match letters on tickets and seats.
- practice writing letter-like forms on tickets.
- respond appropriately to questions.
- pretend to read books on the airplane.

SPOTLIGHT WORDS

airport • country • down • fast • flight attendant • luggage • pilot • runway • slow • state • tickets • traffic control tower • up • USA

MATERIALS

book bags • books • chairs • earphones • food trays • hats • jackets • large blocks • luggage • pencils • posters • row labels

PROPS

- **Airplane Tickets With Seat Assignment** (see page 197 in the Appendix) .
- **Luggage Tag** (see page 197 in the Appendix): Make copies of this page and cut out the airplane tickets and luggage tags for the children to use.

SETTING UP

Encourage the children to use large blocks and chairs to make the inside cabin of an airplane. Put out the airplane props for the children to use. Hang up travel posters of different countries and set up a counter. Let the children hand out tickets and seat assignments. Use letters for the row labels and encourage the children to find their seats by matching the uppercase letters on their tickets to the lowercase letters on their seats. Supply the children with bags of books and magazines to read as they travel to their destination.

OPEN-ENDED QUESTIONS

Where are you going on your airplane?

MAKING BOOKS

▶ **Off on a Trip** (individual or class book): Ask the children who they would take on a trip with them and where they would go. Help the children write their peers' names on their page(s). Point out to the children that names always start with a capital letter. Let the children illustrate the pages. Staple them together to create a book.

EXTENSION ACTIVITIES

1) Help the children make paper airplanes and have a paper airplane toss. Put a hula hoop on the floor and encourage the children to try to throw their airplane in it.
2) Invite a pilot to come in to visit your classroom.
3) Make cloud pictures with cotton balls or white paint. These pictures can be used with the airplane props.

LITERACY RESOURCES—
SONGS, POEMS, AND FINGERPLAYS

Airplane (West and Cox)
There once was a plane in the sky
That took people up very high.
It zoomed through a cloud,
The engine roared loud,
And it flipped and twirled, soaring by.

Airplane Trip (West and Cox)
Quickly we walk up to the gate.
"Hurry! Fast!" we can't be late.
In the plane we find our row.
Buckle our seatbelt before we go!
Tickets and bags we'll have to show.
Through security, I hope you know.
Now everything's ready for us to go.

LITERACY RESOURCES—BOOK LIST

The Airplane Alphabet Book by Jerry Pallotta
Airport by Byron Barton
A Day at the Airport by Richard Scarry
Flying by Donald Crews

Trains

LITERACY APPLICATION: ALLITERATION

Sounds of Letters

Phonemes are individual sounds that correspond to letters. When children isolate the first letter of a word, they learn that particular phoneme. Children begin to connect the letter with the sound. However, this understanding doesn't always occur naturally. Some children need teacher support to help make this connection. Point out and help children group words together that start with the same sound (for example, snake, Sally, silly, and sun). After children have mastered identifying the beginning sound of a word, they can progress to the ending sound. When children begin to read, they must learn to blend phonemes to make a word.

LITERACY OBJECTIVES

Children will:

▶ pretend to read when looking at newspapers and magazines while waiting for the train.

▶ practice writing alphabet letters on tickets.

▶ show phonological awareness by identifying words that start with the same auditory sound.

SPOTLIGHT WORDS

boxcar • coal car • conductor • engine • engineer • gondola • locomotive • railroad tracks

MATERIALS

chairs • dress-up clothes • hats • large blocks • magazines • maps • newspapers • pencils • play money • signs • suitcases • tickets • train books • travel books and brochures • travel games

PROPS

▶ **Train Ticket:** Cut paper into ticket-size squares. Write "Train Ticket" at the top and leave space to write "Cost: $_____" and "Destination: _____" underneath. The children can fill them out and decorate as desired.

SETTING UP

Help the children make a train using large blocks and chairs. If desired, cut out a black silhouette of a train and tape it to the wall. Give the children paper to draw scenery and then attach it to the silhouette for the windows, as if the children are looking through the windows from inside the train. Set up a counter for children to buy tickets and a waiting and reading area. Hang up posters of different destinations. Let the children make signs for the train and to write on the tickets that they are selling. Encourage the children to play games while riding in the train (for example, "I am thinking of something that starts with the letter A…").

OPEN-ENDED QUESTIONS

Where do you want to go on the train?
What is it like to be on a train?

MAKING BOOKS

▶ **Train** (individual book): Make enough copies of the train car pattern (see page 210 in the Appendix) so that each child has a few pages. Ask the children to write what they would see while on a train and illustrate it on the train cars. Help the children spell out some of the words they want to use in their stories by helping them hear the first sound. For example, if the child wants to write: "I saw a river," you could write: "I saw a …" Then, help the child hear the "rrr" sound that starts the word "river" and write it down. This activity helps the children discover that they can figure out what letter a word starts with by sounding it out. Staple all of their pages together to make a book.

EXTENSION ACTIVITIES

1) Help the children hear the beginning sounds of words by using train words such as: smoke stack, train track, loud locomotive, and so on.
2) Go to a train station to see some real trains. Talk about safety at railroad crossings.
3) Talk about model trains and bring one in for the children to see. Encourage the children to make their own floormat track for a model train.

4) Invite a train engineer to come in and talk to the children about what he or she does and to teach the children about different trains and the cars they pull.

LITERACY RESOURCES—
SONGS, POEMS, AND FINGERPLAYS

Clickety Clack (West and Cox)
Clickety clack, clickety clack
A train is coming down the track.
Clickety clack, clickety clack
The whistle blows, I'll soon be back.

Engine, Engine (traditional)
Engine, engine, number nine,
Ring the bell when it's time.
"O-U-T spells out," says he,
Into the middle of the dark blue sea.

Engine, engine, number nine,
Running on the Chicago line.
When she's polished, she will shine.
Engine, engine, number nine,

Engine, engine, number nine,
Running on the Chicago line.
If the train should jump the track,
Do you want your money back?

Engine, engine, number nine,
Running on the Chicago line.
See it sparkle, see it shine,
Engine, engine, number nine.
• For a variation, substitute your own town's name for Chicago.

LITERACY RESOURCES—BOOK LIST

All Aboard Trains by Mary Harding
Big Book of Trains by Christine Heap
Freight Train by Donald Crews
The Little Engine That Could by Watty Piper

Travel

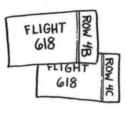

LITERACY APPLICATION

Sharing Books

Give children the opportunity to choose their favorite books
and share them with others. Have a variety of
books available, including those that are
predictable and easy to memorize. This
allows the children to become familiar
and comfortable with the books. It is
exciting to watch children as they read
these books over and over again to
themselves and to their peers. Some
examples of good books are *Polar Bear,
Polar Bear, What Do You Hear?* by Bill Martin
Jr., *The Very Hungry Caterpillar* by Eric Carle, and *Is
Your Mama a Llama?* by Deborah Guarino.

LITERACY OBJECTIVES

Children will:

▶ understand the function of print by seeing and using travel brochures.

▶ pretend to read books while traveling.

▶ carry out a series of directions.

▶ use one object to represent another when writing symbols on a map.

SPOTLIGHT WORDS

close • far • fast • itinerary • long • luggage • map • passport • short • slow
• suitcase • travel • vacation

MATERIALS

books • cameras • chairs • dress-up clothes • large blocks • luggage tags •
maps • play money • pretend video camera • steering wheels • suitcases •
tickets • travel brochures

PROPS

▶ **Passport:** Cut a few pieces of paper in half. Write "Passport" on the
top of each one. Encourage the children to write their names on them
and draw pictures of themselves.

- **Postcard:** Cut cardstock into 3" x 5" rectangles. Add a few lines on the left-hand side for the children to write names and addresses. Encourage the children to decorate the blank side with pictures of vacation spots or landmarks.

SETTING UP

Set out travel props in a large area. Help the children make a car, bus, or airplane using large blocks, chairs, and steering wheels. Then set up a table where the children can fill out passports, tickets, and luggage tags. Put out familiar books for the children to read.

OPEN-ENDED QUESTIONS

What would you take on your trip?
Where will you go on your trip?

MAKING BOOKS

- **Camera** (individual book): Make enough copies of the lens pattern on page 211 in the Appendix so that each child has six circles. Cut them out. Put crayons and six lens circles into zipper-closure plastic bags, one for each child. Give a bag to each child before going on a field trip or outside on a walk. Encourage the children to draw and write what they see on their circles. After you come back, staple the lens circles to the children's camera patterns (see page 211 in the Appendix) to make books. Then encourage the children to share their books with each other at group time.

EXTENSION ACTIVITIES

1) Ask the children to create their own map using symbols.
2) Help the children make an itinerary for their trip. Let the children tell you what they plan to do and then write it down for them.
3) Ask the children to sit in a circle to play this game. Chant, "We're going on a trip, what shall we take?" Go around the circle and let each child take a turn answering the question (for example, a flashlight, a map, cookies, and so on). If needed, brainstorm ahead of time all the things the children could take on a trip to give them some ideas.

LITERACY RESOURCES—
SONGS, POEMS, AND FINGERPLAYS

Transportation (West and Cox)

Cars on the street,
Driving up and down
And all around.
Cars are on the street.

Planes in the air,
Flying up and down
And all around.
Planes are in the air.

Boats on the lake,
Sailing up and down
And all around.
Boats are on the lake.

Trains on the tracks,
Whistling up and down
And all around.
Trains are on the track.

Pack your bag,
Passport in pocket.
Suitcase in hand,
Make sure you lock it.

Its time to take
A little trip.
Out on the dock
And onto the ship.

LITERACY RESOURCES—BOOK LIST

Are We There Yet, Daddy? by Virginia Walters
The Bag I'm Taking to Grandma's by Shirley Neitzel
Emma's Vacation by David McPhail
Me on the Map by Joan Sweeney
Pigs in the Mud in the Middle of the Rud by Lunn Plourde
The Relatives Came by Cynthia Rylant
Simple Pictures Are Best by Nancy Willard
Vroomaloom Zoom by John Coy

Performers

147

Singing

LITERACY APPLICATION

Rhyming

By singing and learning songs, children become familiar with rhyming words. When children produce rhymes, they become phonologically aware of the sounds within words. When children understand the concept that rhyming words are words that sound and often look similar, they learn how to generate words. While rhyming, children can recognize and produce words that are unfamiliar, which helps them with reading and spelling.

LITERACY OBJECTIVES

Children will:

▶ learn to sequence by remembering the words to songs.

▶ follow directions while singing.

▶ expand their vocabulary as they learn new songs.

▶ develop auditory discrimination skills by listening and singing.

▶ begin to recognize some letters.

SPOTLIGHT WORDS

choir • country • director • fast • flat • folk • high • loud • low • note • opera • pitch • sharp • slow • soft • solo

MATERIALS

background music (such as a tape of familiar songs) • batons • blocks • dress-up clothes • microphones • music folders • music stands • programs • sheet music • sign-up list

PROPS

▶ **Music Staff** (see page 198 in the Appendix): Make copies of this page and explain to the children what music notes are. They can use these to make their own "compositions."

SETTING UP

This activity can be set up two different ways: the children can sign up to take turns performing a solo on the stage, or they can take turns being the director and the choir members. Help the children make a stage using large blocks in a large area. Encourage them to set up chairs for the audience and make programs, including the children's names. Then the children can dress up to perform. Play a tape of familiar songs for the children to sing along with or let the children make up their own songs. Encourage them to use their music staffs to pretend to write music.

OPEN-ENDED QUESTIONS

How do you feel when you hear this song?

Does this sound high or low?

Do you like songs that are fast or slow?

Can you think of animals or other living things that like to "sing" in their own ways?

MAKING BOOKS

ABC's for the Piano (individual book): Make copies of the keyboard pages (see pages 212-213 in the Appendix) so that each child gets both pages. Encourage each child to come up with a word that starts with the letter on each piano key. Then, ask them to generate a word that rhymes with it (for example, apple and bapple or betty and getty). Ask the children to write the words and draw pictures on each key. Then, tape the pages together side by side and fold each key back and forth like a fan to make an accordion book. Each piano key is one page of the accordion book.

EXTENSION ACTIVITIES

1) Make a staff on the felt board with moveable notes for the children to experiment with. Talk about what the notes are for and how to use them with music. Teach the children the names of the notes: A, B, C, D, E, F, G. Teach the children about pitch, and help them to discriminate between high and low notes.

2) Present a small concert complete with child-made programs for the children's parents and peers.

3) Clap out the syllables of the children's names while singing.

LITERACY RESOURCES— SONGS, POEMS, AND FINGERPLAYS

My Hat It Has Three Corners (German folk song)
My hat it has three corners,
Three corners has my hat.
And had it not three corners,
It would not be my hat.

Frère Jacques (traditional)
Frère Jacques, Frère Jacques,
Dormez vous? Dormez vous?
Sonnez les matines, sonnez les matines
Ding ding dong, ding ding dong.

English version:
Are you sleeping, are you sleeping?
Brother John, Brother John?
Morning bells are ringing, morning bells are ringing,
Ding ding dong, ding ding dong.

LITERACY RESOURCES—BOOK LIST

Five Little Monkeys Jumping on the Bed by Eileen Christelow
The Itsy, Bitsy Spider by Iza Trapani
Little White Duck by Walt Whippo
Mary Had a Little Lamb by Iza Trapani
There Was an Old Lady Who Swallowed a Fly by Simms Taback
Twinkle, Twinkle Little Star by Iza Trapani

Dance Studio

LITERACY APPLICATION

Listening

Listening to different sounds helps children develop their auditory discrimination skills, which they use when identifying different sounds within words. Rhyming, identifying the first sounds of words, and recognizing sounds through music help children to develop these skills. As children listen to music they also develop an appreciation for sounds, which helps them develop better listening skills. They become more attentive and learn to distinguish between soft, loud, fast, slow, and so on. Listening skills are an important aspect of preparing to read.

LITERACY OBJECTIVES

Children will:

▶ learn rhythm to help them hear syllables (for example, fin-gers or mem-ber-ship).

▶ develop listening skills.

▶ practice writing their names.

SPOTLIGHT WORDS

ankles • arm • down • elbow • fast • fingers • head • knees • legs • movement • neck • rhythm • slow • up

MATERIALS

chairs • dance program • different kinds of dance shoes (ballet, tap, clogs) • labeling cards • large blocks • long mirrors • music • scarves • skirts • streamers • tape recorder • tights

PROPS

▶ **Dance Registration Form** (see page 199 in the Appendix).
▶ **Dance Membership Card** (see page 199 in the Appendix): Make copies of this page and cut out the registration forms and membership cards for the children to use.

SETTING UP

Encourage the children to fill out registration forms and membership cards. Help them make a dance program that lists the performers. Then, encourage the children to make a studio out of large blocks and set up chairs for the audience. Set up several long mirrors around the studio so the children can see themselves dance. Play a variety of music for the children to use while they are dancing. Help the children listen carefully to the music as they dance.

OPEN-ENDED QUESTIONS

Where did you learn to dance?
What kind of dances do you like?
Do you like to dance fast or slow?
What do you think a dancing cow (or other animal) would look like?

MAKING BOOKS

▶ **Dance Stuff** (class book): Give each child a piece of paper. Encourage them to come up with rhyming words for their individual pages about what they would take to dance class (for example, blue shoes or rap tap). It is okay for them to use nonsense words. The children will develop good listening skills by making up words that rhyme.

EXTENSION ACTIVITIES

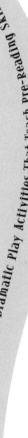

1) Put on a dance recital complete with child-made programs for another class or for parents.
2) Put hula hoops on the floor and have the children dance inside of them. This will teach the children about body space.
3) Do a listening activity by playing different kinds of music and asking the children to express with their bodies how they feel. Let the children take turns guessing how it makes others feel.

LITERACY RESOURCES—
SONGS, POEMS, AND FINGERPLAYS

Skip to My Lou (traditional)
Flies in the buttermilk, shoo, fly, shoo. (skip around in a circle)
Flies in the buttermilk, shoo, fly, shoo.
Flies in the buttermilk, shoo, fly, shoo.
Skip to my Lou, my darlin'.

Chorus:
Skip, skip, skip to my Lou.
Skip, skip, skip to my Lou.
Skip, skip, skip to my Lou.
Skip to my Lou, my darlin'.

Grab your partner, skip to my Lou. (hold both hands or partner)
Grab your partner, skip to my Lou.
Grab your partner, skip to my Lou.
Skip to my Lou, my darlin'.

(chorus)

Lost my partner, what'll I do? (walk around pretending to look for partner)
Lost my partner, what'll I do?
Lost my partner, what'll I do?
Skip to my Lou, my darlin'.

(chorus)

I'll find another one, and it's you.
I'll find another one, and it's you.
I'll find another one, and it's you.
Skip to my Lou, my darlin'.

LITERACY REOURCES—BOOK LIST

Angelina Ballerina by Katherine Holabird
Barn Dance by John Archambault
Boogie Bones by Elizabeth Loredo
Clap Your Hands by Lorinda Bryan Cauley
Hop Jump by Ellen Stoll Walsh
Jiggle Wiggle Prance by Sally Noll
Max by Rachel Isadora
Nina, Nina, Ballerina by Jane O'Connor
Saturday Night at the Dinosaur Stomp by Carol Diggory Shields
Shake My Sillies Out by Raffi
The Twelve Dancing Princesses by the Grimm Brothers

Art Gallery

LITERACY APPLICATION

Writing Oral Language Promotes Creativity

When children are enthusiastic about their artwork, they want to verbalize it with others. It is important to let them dictate or write down how they perceive their own pieces of art. As children create and title their work they develop confidence in themselves. It is important not to tell children what to write (for example, "You drew a pretty flower; why don't you call it the flower picture?"). This stifles their creativity. Instead, it is important to encourage creativity by supporting and writing down children's ideas.

LITERACY OBJECTIVES

Children will:

▶ begin to write words with adult help.
▶ be involved in creative writing.

SPOTLIGHT WORDS

art • bright • color • dark • design • dull • form • hue • light • line • size • texture

MATERIALS

banner • cardboard easels • certificates • chalk • clipboards • collage material • colored pencils • judging checklist • label cards • paint • paper • playdough • ribbons • tickets • title tags • watercolors

PROPS

▶ **Artwork Label Cards**: Draw borders around index cards and write "Title of Artwork" at the top. The children can use these to label their works of art.

▶ **Award**: Draw a trophy or ribbon shape and write "Award for _____" at the top. Make a few copies and cut them out. The judges can use these to write the child's name and what the award is for (prettiest flower, most original, and so on).

SETTING UP

▶ Before the children can create an art gallery on their own, you will need to explain what an art gallery is and take them to an art show, if possible.

▶ Collect the children's artwork after they have titled and signed their work. Mount the children's artwork on poster board and hang in the room or hallway. Encourage the children to make banners announcing and advertising their art gallery. Let the children take turns judging their peers' artwork. Talk about some basic rules before you let the children be judges and make sure they understand that they can only say positive things about the artwork. Choose two children at a time to work together as judges and ask them to judge a couple of pieces of artwork. This allows everyone an opportunity to be a judge. Give the judges clipboards on which to write their results. The children can come up with awards for each art piece, such as the greenest picture, the prettiest flower, the rainbow picture, and so on.

OPEN-ENDED QUESTIONS

What makes this picture special?
Can you tell me about your picture?
What is different about this picture?
What is your favorite thing about this picture?

MAKING BOOKS

▶ **Feelings** (individual book): On several pages, write "_____ (color) makes me feel _____." Make enough copies so that each child gets all the pages. Encourage the children to express how different colors make them feel. Make sure to validate whatever they say in a positive way; feelings are very personal and can be fragile. Write down what they say on their pages and let them illustrate them.

If desired, do just one page a day so there is more time to talk about feelings. When children are encouraged to express their feelings and see them written down, it helps to validate them and build self-esteem. As their confidence grows, their creativity will be enhanced.

EXTENSION ACTIVITIES

1) Teach the children about different kinds of art, such as watercolors, oil, pencil drawings, and so on. Show the children different pictures of classical art created with these materials.

2) Invite an artist to come into the classroom and paint or sculpt in front of the children.

LITERACY RESOURCES—SONGS, POEMS, AND FINGERPLAYS

A Rainbow of Colors (West and Cox)
Green as the grass between my toes,
Yellow as the sun on my nose.

Blue as the sky without a cloud,
Purple as violets I once found.

Red as an apple just picked for me,
Orange as a sunset sinking in the sea.

LITERACY RESOURCES—BOOK LIST

Color Farm by Lois Ehlert
A Color of His Own by Leo Lionni
Color Zoo by Lois Ehlert
Harold and the Purple Crayon by Crokett Johnson
In the Garden With Van Gogh by Julie Merberg, Suzanne Bober
Little Blue and Little Yellow by Leo Lionni
A Magical Day With Matisse by Julie Merberg, Suzanne Bober
Mouse Paint by Ellen Stoll Walsh
My Many Colored Days by Dr. Seuss
A Picture for Harold's Room by Crokett Johnson
White Rabbit's Color Book by Alan Baker

Blue
makes me feel
Quiet
and peaceful.

Yellow
makes me feel
Happy

Purple
makes me feel
silly

Olympics
(Track and Field)

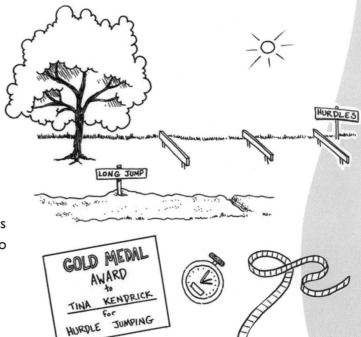

LITERACY APPLICATION

Using Forms for Recording Information

Children often are excited to record information in their own books. This even motivates children who do not usually like to write. For some children this will be their first attempt to write. It is important to give children opportunities to write in a comfortable and secure environment.

LITERACY OBJECTIVES

Children will:

◗ practice writing when they record information in record books.

◗ recognize and write their names on certificates and record sheets.

◗ understand the meaning of print by making and reading the labeled event cards.

SPOTLIGHT WORDS

endurance • events • exercise • far • finish • long • near • Olympics • short • sportsmanship • start

MATERIALS

certificates • hurdles (low to the ground) • labels for events • measuring tape • paper plates (for discus throw) • sand pile (for the long jump) • sticks (for javelin throwing) • stop watches

PROPS

◗ **Award:** Draw a blue ribbon and write "Kid's Olympic Award" on it. Leave a space for the child's name and event.

SETTING UP

Set up the different track and field events on the playground, in a park, or in a field with a track. Label the different events with signs. Events could include the discus toss (paper plate), the long jump (measuring tape, small marking flags, rake, and sand pile), the javelin throw (long stick, small marking cones, and measuring tape), sprinting, and hurdles (small boxes). Encourage the children to record their own results in their "Kids' Olympics" book (see Making Books below). Let the children create awards for each other and give them out to everyone who participates.

OPEN-ENDED QUESTIONS

What event would you like to be involved in?
What are your goals?
How will you meet your goals?

MAKING BOOKS

▶ **Kids' Olympics** (individual book): Draw a horizontal and a vertical line through the middle of a piece of paper to divide it into four quarters. Do this on another sheet, so that you have eight squares. Write one of the following items in each square:

> *My Record Book! Created by:* _____
> *I can throw the shot-put* _____ *feet.*
> *I can throw a discus* _____ *feet.*
> *I can throw a javelin* _____ *feet.*
> *I can climb* _____ *stairs.*
> *I can jump* _____ *feet.*
> *I can run* _____ *yards.*
> *I can jump* _____ *hurdles.*

Make copies of the two pages and cut them into quarters to make an eight-page book for each child. Staple the pages together. The children can use these books to measure and record their performance in each event. Encourage the children to write at their developmental level—even separate marks with beginning forms should be validated. Ask them to illustrate the events on each page.

EXTENSION ACTIVITIES

1) Show the children flags from different countries and explain how they are used during the Olympics.

2) Talk about the training that Olympic athletes must do. Ask the children to make up their own training schedule by listing different activities or exercises on a chart. Encourage them to keep track of their progress.

LITERACY RESOURCES—SONGS, POEMS, AND FINGERPLAYS

Olympics (West and Cox)
Swimming and jumping,
Running galore.
All this is what
The Olympics are for.

Medals (West and Cox)
One, two, three
Olympic medals for me.
Bronze, silver, gold,
Which one will I hold?

LITERACY RESOURCES—BOOK LIST

The Hare and the Tortoise by Carol Jones
What's Faster Than a Speeding Cheetah? by Robert E. Wells

Theater

LITERACY APPLICATION

Retelling a Story

Retelling stories helps children gain an understanding of basic story elements, which is essential to reading comprehension. As children act out books, they gain an understanding of the story line. They see that books follow a sequence and that there is a beginning, middle, and an end to a story. Encourage them to talk about their favorite part or character, predict what might come next, and discuss how they feel about the story. This activity helps the children learn the value of reading and gain an appreciation and love for books.

LITERACY OBJECTIVES

Children will:
▶ pretend to read the books they act out.
▶ develop reading comprehension skills as they act out books.
▶ be able to sequence the series of events in the book they act out.
▶ see books as being enjoyable and have a desire to learn to read.

SPOTLIGHT WORDS

actor • after • audience • before • beginning • characters • director • editor • end • middle • next • performance • play • props • scene • scenery • script • wardrobe

MATERIALS

chairs • costumes • props that go along with the book • puppet stage or large blocks • puppets • several copies of the same book • signs

SETTING UP

Choose a familiar book that has a simple story line, such as *Goldilocks and The Three Bears* or *Where the Wild Things Are* by Maurice Sendak. Read the book to the children several times and have it available for the children to read. If the children have not acted out a book before, model how to do it. For example, present a puppet show to the children using the book you have chosen, role play the different parts in the story, and demonstrate how to use different voices and be expressive. When the children are confident with the story line in the book, they will be ready to create their own play. Encourage them to take on different roles within the story. Have props and costumes available for the children to use, and if desired, let them make scenery. Make sure that the book is part of the props and encourage the children to take the part of the narrator as other children act out the story. The children can also act out the story using puppets. Use a puppet stage or large blocks to make a stage and set up chairs for the audience. Help the children make signs announcing their play, tickets, and programs. Encourage the children to take turns being the audience or the actors. This activity can be as involved or as simple as you want. If desired, the children can present their play to another class or their parents.

OPEN-ENDED QUESTIONS

What kind of clothes will you need?
What will happen in your play?
How will your play begin?
How will it end?
What will the characters say?
What kind of scenery will you need?

MAKING BOOKS

▸ **Scroll Book** (class book): Beforehand, make a scroll box using a large box, scissors or craft knife, and two wooden dowels. Cut a large opening in the bottom of a box, leaving about a 1" frame around the hole (like a screen). Make four round holes (the same diameter as the dowels) in the frame of the box, two on the top and two on the bottom. Slide the dowels through the holes. Give the children a roll of paper and encourage them to write and illustrate their play on it. Attach the paper to the dowels and let the children roll it through. Then give them the opportunity to retell their stories to each other.

EXTENSION ACTIVITIES

1) Help the children make the scenery and props for the play. Have them work in groups or assign jobs.
2) Take the children to see a play. If possible, set up a time to go backstage and talk to the actors and see the scenery, costumes, and set.
3) Encourage the children to make up a script.

LITERACY RESOURCES— SONGS, POEMS, AND FINGERPLAYS

A Melodrama (West and Cox)
I'm excited to share with you
Two tickets I have for the play.
I can hardly wait to see who
Will play the villain today.

The hero is surely to be
The one who saves the day.
A heroine will be set free
As we sing and shout hooray!

LITERACY RESOURCES—BOOK LIST

Anansi and the Moss-Covered Rock by Eric A. Kimmel
Go Away Big Green Monster by Ed Emberley
I Went Walking by Sue Williams
King Bidgood's in the Bathtub by Audrey Wood
The Mitten by Jan Brett
The Wide Mouthed Frog by Keith Faulkner
Where the Wild Things Are by Maurice Sendak

Reading, Writing, and Talking

Newspaper
Collecting Meaningful Information

Post office
Invented Spellings

Library
Handling a Book

School
ABC Manipulatives Teach Letter Knowledge

Nursery Rhymes
Onset Rhyme Blending

Office
Purposeful Conversation

Newspaper

LITERACY APPLICATION

Collecting Meaningful Information

As children collect information that is meaningful to them for their own newspaper, they are more motivated to write. For example, if a child is excited about sports or weather, she will want to find information for that section of the newspaper. This activity helps children learn how to organize their thoughts and write them down. You can use this opportunity to model writing as the children dictate their collected information, which helps them see that print has meaning. When children are able to see and read their completed product, they are motivated to become readers and writers—an essential and exciting part of beginning literacy.

LITERACY OBJECTIVES

Children will:

▶ see that words can be written as they dictate their findings.

▶ see that print has meaning when they make a newspaper.

▶ understand that books are used to find information.

SPOTLIGHT WORDS

advertisement • article • editor • investigate • newspaper • photographer • recycle • report • reporter • weather

MATERIALS

clipboards • newspapers • old cameras • old computer keyboards • paper • pencils • telephones

SETTING UP

▶ Before setting up a newsroom, do the following activity so that children understand the concepts required to create a newspaper. Teach the children about newspapers. Collect newspapers and let the children look at them in the classroom. Keep copies in your book area for several weeks.

▶ After the children know what a newspaper is, help them create their own newspaper. Split the children into groups and assign an adult to each group. (You may need to invite parents to help out.) Give each group a topic such as sports, weather, education, environment, people, or favorite books. Give them clipboards to record their findings and a camera to take pictures. The children can draw pictures of what they see on their clipboards and dictate their findings to the adult in their group. They could interview a classmate, visit a business nearby, observe events outside their school, or make a weather station. Then, they should come back and write their findings with adult help. The teacher will then compile their reports and make copies. The children can give copies of their newspaper to their parents, other classes, teachers, and so on.

OPEN-ENDED QUESTIONS

Where does paper come from?
What can you do with paper?
What happened?
What will you report on?
How do you create a newspaper?

MAKING BOOKS

▶ **Newspaper** (class book): Make a weekly class newspaper with the children using the pattern on page 214 in the Appendix. After a few weeks, put all the pages together to make a book. When children read the information they have compiled, it is very meaningful to them.

EXTENSION ACTIVITIES

1) Have a "tree" party. Encourage the children to make invitations, and then plant a tree in your playground. Talk to the children about the importance of recycling.

2) Encourage the children to make a book about all the different things a tree can be used for, such as swinging, shade, a bird's nest, and so on.

3) Visit a newspaper and talk to a reporter about how articles are written.

LITERACY RESOURCES— SONGS, POEMS, AND FINGERPLAYS

Newspaper (West and Cox)
(Tune: "The Farmer in the Dell")
The reporter gets the news,
The reporter gets the news.
Hi, ho, the reporter,
The reporter gets the news.

The photographer takes the picture,
The photographer takes the picture.
Hi, ho, the photographer,
The photographer takes the picture.

The children read the news,
The children read the news.
Hi, ho, the children,
The children read the news.

Newspapers (West and Cox)
Newspaper, black and white,
Newspaper, rolled up tight.

Newspaper, thrown with care,
Newspaper, lands on the stair.

Newspaper, I will see,
Newspaper, delivered to me.

LITERACY RESOURCES—BOOK LIST

Deadline!: From News to Newspaper by Gail Gibbons
From Tree to Paper by Pam Marshall
The Furry News, How to Make a Newspaper by Loreen Leedy
The Giving Tree by Shel Silverstein
The Paperboy by Dav Pilkey

Post Office

LITERACY APPLICATION

Invented Spellings

It is important to support children's attempts as they invent spellings; however, teachers often feel that children will learn bad habits if they allow this. This is a false concept. When children are beginning to write, they need to feel confident. Teachers can expose the children to correct spellings by responding to children's requests to spell a word while they are writing letters. Correct spellings will come as their phonological awareness increases.

LITERACY OBJECTIVES

Children will:

▸ learn the difference between writing and drawing by writing notes to their friends.

▸ match letters and words while sorting mail and writing notes to their friends.

SPOTLIGHT WORDS

address • card • deliver • envelopes • mail carrier • mailbox • note • package • post master • post office • sorting • stamps

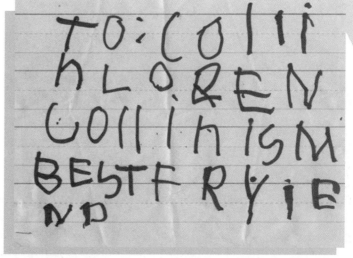

MATERIALS

class address book • envelopes • FedEx boxes and pouches • label stickers for addresses • mail bags • mail carrier hats and shirts • mail sorter trays • mailboxes • name cards • "Open" and "Closed" signs • paper • pencils • play money • stamps (cut them off of mailed envelopes or use junk mail stamps) • stationery

PROPS

▶ **Sample Letter**: Type up a sample letter, with the date, address, salutation, body text, and closing on it. Encourage the children to use it as a model to write their own letters.

SETTING UP

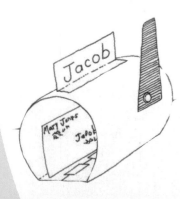

Put the post office props in the dramatic play area. Encourage the children to write letters to each other. Make sure you have name cards for the children to use. If asked, help the children with the correct spelling of words. Make a mailbox for each child by rolling up a piece of paper and taping it together. Then crease one side so it is flat on the bottom. Attach the children's names to their boxes and let them find their own mailboxes to get their letters. Help the children do different jobs at the post office, such as sorting the mail, putting the mail into the mailboxes, selling stamps, and delivering mail.

OPEN-ENDED QUESTIONS

Whom will you write to?
What do you want to write?

MAKING BOOKS

▶ **Letters** (individual book): Read *The Jolly Postman* by Janet and Allan Ahlberg to the children and talk about writing letters to other people. Tape real envelopes on pieces of paper. Give each child a few sheets of plain paper, as well as a few envelope pages. Ask the children to write letters to different people and then put them in the envelopes. Encourage the children to spell out words themselves. Put all the pages together to make a book.

EXTENSION ACTIVITIES

1) Go on a field trip to the post office. Learn about the different jobs people do there and how mail is delivered. Or, invite a mail carrier to visit your classroom.

2) Ask the children to write a note to someone and then take it to the post office to mail. Let them buy their own stamps.

3) Go on a mailbox hunt. Go for a walk in the neighborhood and look at mailboxes. Encourage the children to look for different kinds of mailboxes in their own neighborhoods and take pictures of them or draw what they look like. Then let them share their findings with others in the class.

LITERACY RESOURCES— SONGS, POEMS, AND FINGERPLAYS

A Letter (West and Cox)
(Tune: "A Tisket, a Tasket")
A letter, a letter,
I can send a letter.
I write a note and stamp it, too,
And put it in the mailbox.

E-mail, e-mail,
I can write an e-mail.
I type it in and click the mouse,
And send it to my friend.

A Special Note (West and Cox)
A special note I wrote today,
Sits in an envelope that I'll send away.

I licked the edge and closed it tight,
Making sure it's sealed just right.

Put on a stamp and address it to
Someone special, can you guess who?

LITERACY RESOURCES—BOOK LIST

Dear Annie by Judith Caseley
Messages in the Mailbox: How to Write a Letter by Loreen Leedy
The Post Office Book: Mail and How It Moves by Gail Gibbons
Tortoise Brings the Mail by Dee Lillegard

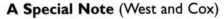

Reading, Writing, and Talking

Library

LITERACY APPLICATION

Handling a Book

It is important to teach children what a book is, how to handle books appropriately and respectfully, and how to be an author and illustrator. The library is one of the places where children learn these skills.

Children should be able to understand what the beginning and end of a story are, and what will happen next. They also should understand the difference between pictures and words and identify the front and back of a book.

LITERACY OBJECTIVES

Children will:

▶ pretend to read and write.
▶ associate books with reading.
▶ learn that print goes from left to right and front to back.
▶ learn what an author and illustrator are.
▶ learn the different parts of a book such as pages, title, front, back, illustrations, print, and so on.
▶ enjoy reading.

SPOTLIGHT WORDS

books • catalogue • check out • due • fables • fairy tales • fiction • folk tales • librarian • library card • magazines • newspapers • non-fiction • reading

MATERIALS

beanbag chairs • book cards • book markers • books • bookshelves • calendars • date stamp • magazines • newspapers • "Open" and "Closed" signs • posters of favorite books and authors • stamp pad

PROPS

▶ **Library Cards:** Make library cards on small squares of paper. Write the name of your school and library and leave a space for the child's name.

- **Due Date Cards:** Turn an index card lengthwise and write the name of your school and library at the top. Write "Date" underneath. Divide the card into two columns. The children can use these to stamp due dates on.
- **Bookworm** (see page 200 in the Appendix): Make copies of the pattern and give a few to each child (you only need one copy of the face portion, but many copies of the body portion). Ask the children to keep track of the books they read with their parents during the week. Write them on the bookworm (body portion) and hang them in the classroom.

Green Meadows School Library	
Date	
Oct. 4, 2003	
Nov. 14, 2003	
Dec. 6, 2003	

SETTING UP

Create a library in a large area of your classroom, such as the block area. (Don't use your book area because it is important to keep a quiet, secluded area in the classroom for those children who may need quiet time.) Make a check-out counter using a table or blocks and stock it with a stamp pad, date stamp, calendar, and due date cards. Arrange books, newspapers, and magazines on bookshelves. Hang up posters and put out bean bag chairs to make a cozy place to read. Encourage the children to write their names on library cards and make "Open" and "Closed" signs.

OPEN-ENDED QUESTIONS

What kinds of books do you like to read?
What is your favorite part?
Which pictures do you like?

MAKING BOOKS

- **Mr. Wiggly, the Book Worm** (individual book): Read *Mr. Wiggle Goes to the Library* by Paula Craig to the children and talk about how to respect books. Encourage the children to make up their own stories about Mr. Wiggly (the bookworm) and illustrate them. Staple their pages together to make books.
- **Name Book** (individual book): Use the letters of each child's name to make individual books. Write one letter on each of the child's pages. Encourage the children to come up with different words that start with the letters in their names. You or the child can write the words on the page. Explain that the words should be things that reflect the children and their interests (an example is on the following page).

K: kite, kitten
A: angel, apricots, apples
T: tie shoes, tap dance
E: elephant, egg

A child's own name is very special to her. When the child is encouraged to be the author and illustrator of her own book, she begins to understand what that means. It also creates the perfect opportunity to teach children the sequence of a book: that there is a beginning, middle, and an end.

EXTENSION ACTIVITIES

1) Go to a library during reading time. Ask the librarian to talk about how to respect books. Let the children check out their own books to keep in the classroom.

2) Explain to the children what an author and illustrator are. Encourage them to write their own stories and illustrate them. Choose a good, predictable book that children can add on to. Also show them how to do special illustrations, such as Eric Carle does with collages.

3) Invite a local author or illustrator to come in and show his or her books or pictures to the children.

4) Let the children make their own bookmarks.

5) Encourage each child to share her favorite book with the class. Ask the child to explain why it is her favorite book.

6) Teach the children about sign language and Braille. Bring in a book written in Braille for the children to feel. These can be found in your local library.

LITERACY RESOURCES— SONGS, POEMS, AND FINGERPLAYS

From A to Z (West and Cox)
From A to Z,
Look and see.
I'll find a book
Just right for me.
Search and find
From A to Z.
Search and find
A book for me.

Books (West and Cox)
Books are what I like to read.
They make me laugh and cry and sing.
Little books are what I need
To bring life into everything.

LITERACY RESOURCES—BOOK LIST

The Baby Beebee Bird by Diane Redfield Massie

Brown Bear, Brown Bear, What Do You See? by Bill Martin Jr.

Check It Out!: The Book About Libraries by Gail Gibbons

Dinosaur Roar by Paul and Henrietta Stickland

In the Small, Small Pond by Denise Fleming

Inside a Barn in the Country by Alyssa Satin Capucilli

If You Give a Moose a Muffin by Laura Numeroff

Mr. Wiggle's Book by Paula Craig

My Friend Bear by Jez Alborough

The Napping House by Audrey Wood

One Duck Stuck by Phyllis Root

Polar Bear, Polar Bear, What Do You Hear? by Bill Martin, Jr.

The Selfish Crocodile by Faustin Charles

Silly Sally by Audrey Wood

Tumble Bumble by Felicia Bond

The Very Busy Spider by Eric Carle

The Very Hungry Caterpillar by Eric Carle

The Very Quiet Cricket by Eric Carle

Where the Wild Things Are by Maurice Sendak

School

LITERACY APPLICATION

ABC Manipulatives Teach Letter Knowledge

Young children learn best with hands-on activities where they can manipulate and experiment with objects. Often, the letters of the alphabet are taught using worksheets; however, these can be very abstract for children and can actually defeat the purpose for which they were made. Fortunately, there are many concrete and appropriate alternatives to teaching the alphabet. Try using magnetic letters, sandpaper letters, flannel letters, wooden letters, foam letters, letter blocks, letter matching games, and other manipulatives in the classroom. Children can use these types of manipulatives when playing school.

LITERACY OBJECTIVES

Children will:

▶ pretend to read and write.
▶ recognize and write their names on an attendance chart.
▶ recognize different letters while using manipulatives.
▶ enjoy learning to read and write.

SPOTLIGHT WORDS

homework • principal • recess • rules • student • teacher

MATERIALS

ABC manipulatives (magnetic letters, wooden letter blocks, alphabet puzzles, sponge letters, sandpaper letters, die-cut letters) • alphabet and number books • books • calendar • chairs • chalk and small chalk boards • desks • dry erase markers and boards • erasers • name tags • number and letter posters • paper • pencils • rulers • scissors

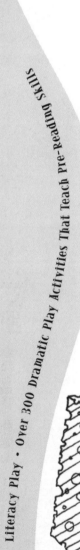

PROPS

▶ **Attendance Chart:** Write "Attendance" at the top of a sheet of lined paper. The children can use this to write their names while taking attendance.

SETTING UP

Set up the dramatic play area to look like a schoolroom with desks, school supplies, and charts on the walls. Select the ABC manipulatives you think will work best with the children. Encourage the children to take on the roles of the teacher or students. Ask them to write their names on the attendance chart. Encourage the children to pretend to read and write during school. As the children play, talk about school in positive ways.

OPEN-ENDED QUESTIONS

What will you learn in school today?
What does the teacher do?
What is your favorite part of school?

MAKING BOOKS

▶ **ABC's** (class book): Write each letter of the alphabet on sheets of paper (one letter per page) and place them inside clear cover sheets in a three-ring binder. Ask the children to find pictures of things that start with each letter of the alphabet. They can bring pictures from home. Encourage the children to make a collage with the pictures on the correct page.

▶ **Chalk Board** (individual book): Give each child a few pieces of black construction paper. Encourage the children to use chalk to draw and write different words that start with each letter of the alphabet. Encourage the children to come up with their own titles and stories. Staple all the pages together to make books.

EXTENSION ACTIVITIES

1. Bring your preschoolers to visit a kindergarten room and talk about school in positive ways. Talk about normal kindergarten routines and rules.

LITERACY RESOURCES— SONGS, POEMS, AND FINGERPLAYS

On My Teacher's Desk (West and Cox)

Pencil,

And paper,

And chalk so white.

Ruler,

And teacher,

And my ABC's right.

LITERACY RESOURCES—BOOK LIST

A Is for...? A Photographer's Alphabet of Animals by Henry Horenstein

Alpha Bugs by David A. Carter

Miss Bindergarten Gets Ready for Kindergarten by Joseph Slate

The Butterfly Alphabet by Kjell B. Sandved

Chicka Chicka Boom Boom by Bill Martin, Jr.

Dr. Seuss's ABC by Dr. Seuss

Eating the Alphabet by Lois Ehlert

Froggy Goes to School by Jonathan London

Handsigns: A Sign Language Alphabet by Kathleen Fain

The Kissing Hand by Audrey Penn

Will I Have a Friend? by Miriam Cohen

Nursery Rhymes

LITERACY APPLICATION

Onset Rhyme Blending

When children are exposed to literature such as nursery rhymes, they hear rhyming words. This provides the opportunity to point out what makes a rhyming word and how rhyming words can be put together into "word families." For example, when the children read "Jack and Jill," point out that "Jill" and "hill" are rhyming words because the first letters and sounds of the words are different (J and H), but the ending sounds are the same (ill). Then, help the children find other words that would belong together to make a word family (such as Bill, till, and mill). This helps children learn that when they change the first letter or sound of a word, they are creating a new word. When children create new rhyming words, they are blending new sounds together. This is an important step to being able to phonetically hear a word—a critical skill for reading.

LITERACY OBJECTIVES

Children will:
- understand what rhyming is.
- reenact nursery rhymes.
- develop oral discrimination as they listen for rhyming words.
- stop and listen to each other as they rhyme with the teacher.
- use pencils, crayons, and paper to illustrate nursery rhymes.

SPOTLIGHT WORDS

Emphasize all of the rhyming words in each nursery rhyme the children learn.

MATERIALS

Collect materials that relate to the nursery rhyme being reenacted. For example, for "Humpty Dumpty," put out papier-mâché eggs, large classroom blocks, stick horses, a crown, and a fancy cloth draped over a chair to make a throne. For "Jack and Jill," put out pails, funny hats and scarves, and classroom blocks.

PROPS

▶ **Word Cards**: Make word cards with rhyming words and matching pictures for each nursery rhyme you use.

SETTING UP

▶ Before doing this dramatic play activity, the children should already know some nursery rhymes. To teach the nursery rhymes, put nursery rhyme books in your library area. Over a period of time, help the children memorize different nursery rhymes. Make poster-size flip charts for each nursery rhyme you teach, as well as word cards with pictures of the rhyming words in the nursery rhymes.

When the children are familiar with some of the nursery rhymes, they can reenact some of them in dramatic play. Following are some examples:

• "Humpty Dumpty": Help the children make papier-mâché eggs and use large classroom blocks to make a wall. The king can wear a crown and sit on a throne, and the king's men can use stick horses.

• "Jack and Jill": Put out pails and funny hats for the children to wear going "up the hill." Help them make a pretend well out of classroom blocks.

OPEN-ENDED QUESTIONS

▶ Ask any open-ended questions that relate to the nursery rhyme being used. For example:

How do you think Jack and Jill felt?

What did Jack and Jill do after they fell down the hill?

How did the king feel after Humpty Dumpty fell off the wall and they couldn't put him back together again?

MAKING BOOKS

▶ **Our Favorite Nursery Rhymes** (class book): Help each child write her favorite nursery rhyme on a page and ask her to illustrate it. Compile all the pages together to make a class book. When reading the book out loud, emphasize the family word rhymes, such as "Jill" and "hill" in "Jack and Jill."

EXTENSION ACTIVITIES

1) Invite a librarian to visit and tell nursery rhymes to the children.
2) Dress up like Mother Goose and tell the children the background history of nursery rhymes.

LITERACY RESOURCES— SONGS, POEMS, AND FINGERPLAYS

Jack and Jill (traditional)
Jack and Jill went up a hill
To fetch a pail of water.
Jack fell down and broke his crown,
And Jill came tumbling after.

Humpty Dumpty (traditional)
Humpty Dumpty sat on a wall,
Humpty Dumpty had a great fall.
All the king's horses and all the king's men
Couldn't put Humpty together again.

LITERACY RESOURCES—BOOK LIST

A Child's Treasury of Nursery Rhymes by Kady MacDonald Denton (Illustrator)
Grandmother's Nursery Rhymes/Las Nanas De Abuelita by Nelly Palacio Jaramillo
Hey, Diddle Diddle (Extended Nursery Rhymes) by Kin Eagle
Humpty Dumpty (Extended Nursery Rhymes) by Kin Eagle
Jack and Jill and Big Dog Bill: A Phonics Reader (Step into Reading) by Martha Weston
Richard Scarry's Mother Goose Rhymes and Nursery Tales by Richard Scarry

Office

LITERACY APPLICATION

Purposeful Conversations

Developing oral language is a precursor to reading and writing. Children should be involved in informal conversations on a daily basis. Using language in a variety of ways supports children's knowledge and vocabulary development. Using telephones motivates children who normally do not talk much.

LITERACY OBJECTIVES

Children will:

▶ learn to recognize and write their peer's names in the class telephone book.

▶ understand the meaning of print as they write notes.

▶ match letters to beginning sounds as they look up each other's telephone number.

SPOTLIGHT WORDS

conversation • file • fold • list • message • office • staple • telephone

MATERIALS

blank calendar • class telephone book • empty stapler • file folders • message pads • paper • paper clips • paper sorter • pencil holders • pencils • tape • telephone books • telephones

SETTING UP

Set up the dramatic play area to look like an office. Put out the props and encourage the children to pretend to read and write messages. Make a class telephone book for the children to use (see Making Books on the following page). Write each child's name on a separate card and glue her photo to it. The children can file the cards by the first letter in the child's name.

OPEN-ENDED QUESTIONS

Who are you going to call today?
What letter file should you put that card under?

MAKING BOOKS

▶ **Telephone Book** (class book): Give each child a piece of paper. Take a photo of each child, help the children fill in their name and phone number on their paper, and then ask them to glue their picture on their paper. Staple all the pages together to make a book. When finished, let the children use it as a prop in their telephone office. This book motivates the children to pretend to call others on the phone and have conversations. You can use this class telephone book with many different dramatic play props.

EXTENSION ACTIVITIES

1) Visit an office and find out what the administrative assistant does.
2) Help the children make their own telephones out of boxes. Draw the number buttons so the children can practice dialing their own phone number.

LITERACY RESOURCES—
SONGS, POEMS, AND FINGERPLAYS

Call a Friend (West and Cox)
(Tune: "Row, Row, Row Your Boat")
Call, call, call a friend
Friend, I'm calling you.

Hi, hello, how are you?
Very well, thank you!

LITERACY RESOURCES—BOOK LIST

Impatient Pamela Calls 911 by Mary Koski
Telephone by Jamey Gambrell

Appendix

Props

Making Books

A

T D

Q N Y C S

V F U P J Z

R G E H T

B W X K L I M O N

DETECTIVE

Firefighter

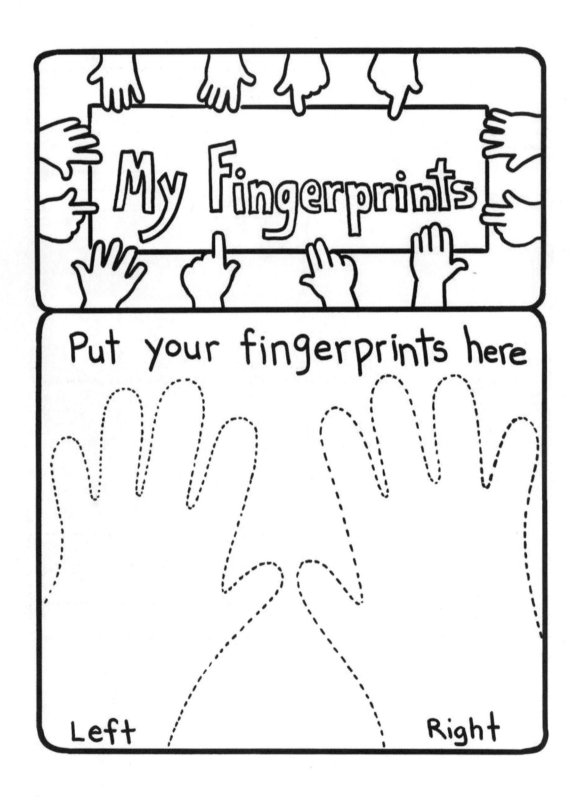

My Fingerprints

Put your fingerprints here

Left   Right

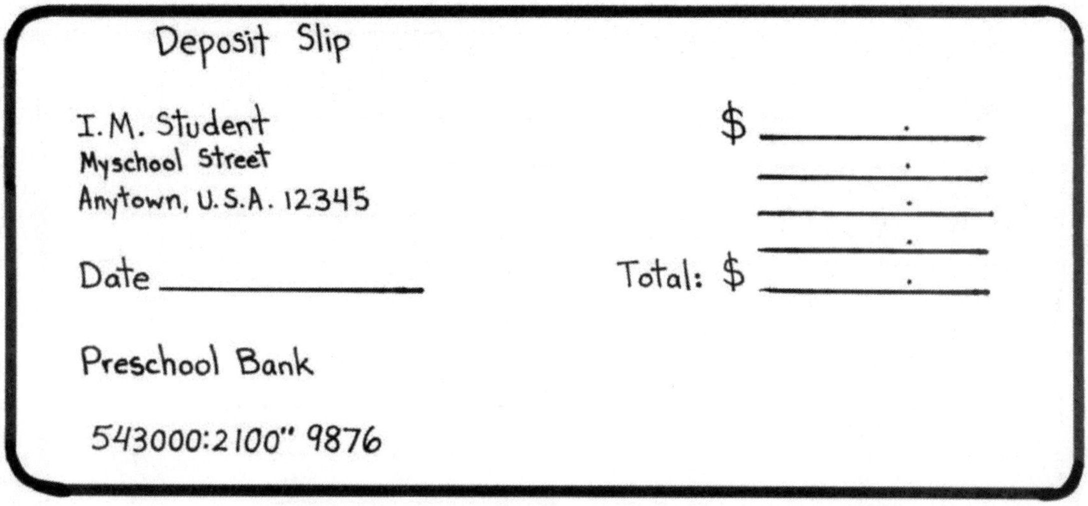

Deposit Slip

I. M. Student
Myschool Street
Anytown, U.S.A. 12345

$ _____ . _____

_____ . _____

_____ . _____

Date _____

_____ . _____

Total: $ _____ . _____

Preschool Bank

543000:2100" 9876

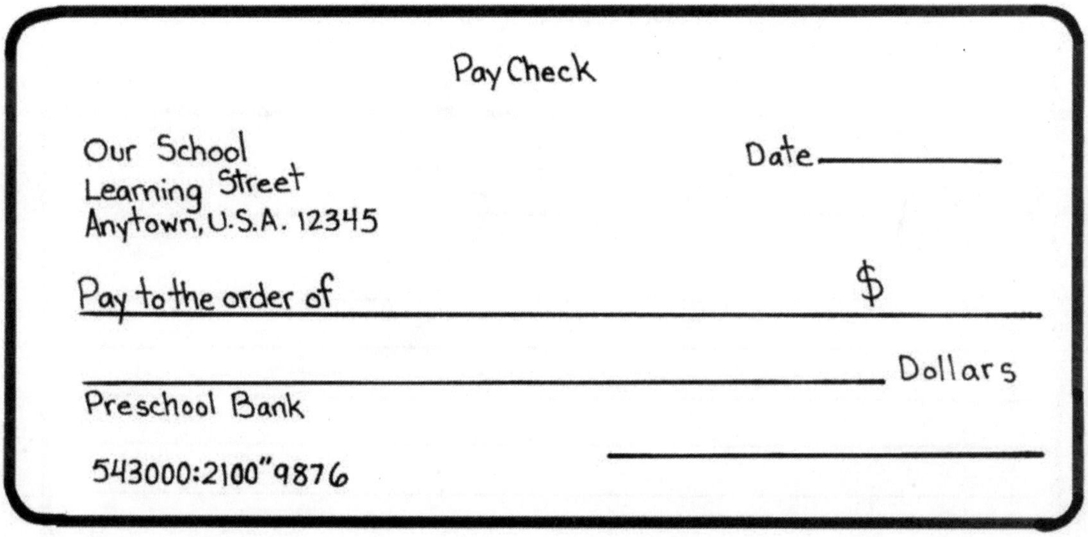

Pay Check

Our School
Learning Street
Anytown, U.S.A. 12345

Date _____

Pay to the order of _____ $ _____

_____ Dollars

Preschool Bank

543000:2100"9876

_____

© Gryphon House, Inc. • 800.638.0928 • www.gryphonhouse.com

Recipe

Recipe

snake

Deer tracks

Skunk

fox

porcupine

Bear

bird

Bear tracks

Racoon

moose

tent

bugs

Picnic List

 Basket

 Napkin

 Lemonade

 Cup

 Fork and Spoon

 Watermelon

 Hamburger

 Hot Dog

 Corn Chips

 Ice Cream

 Plate

 Ants

Guest Check ☕

Check Number
123456

		AMOUNT
	TAX	
	TOTAL	

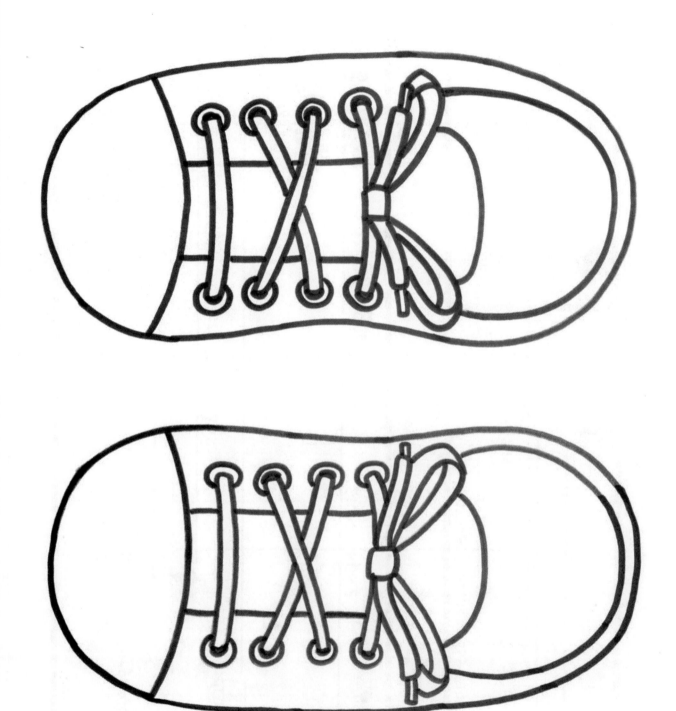

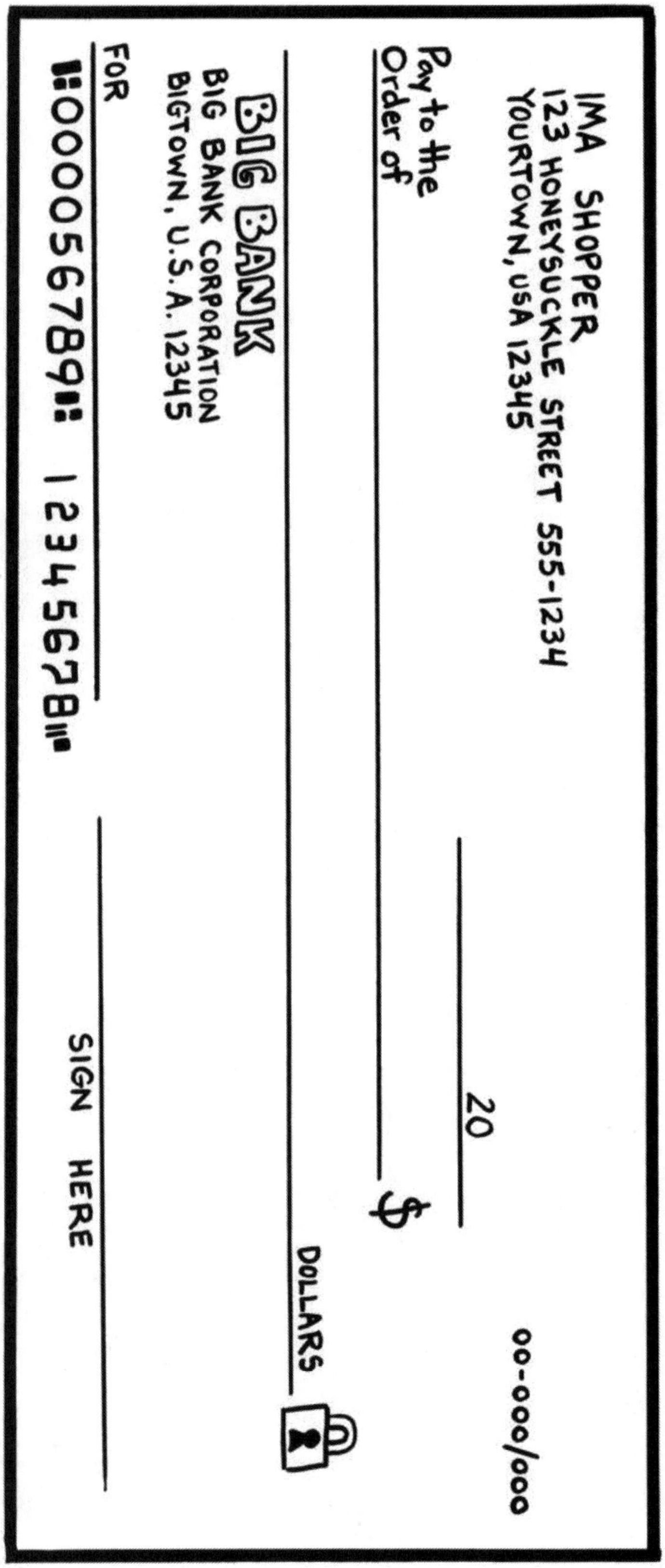

IMA SHOPPER
123 HONEYSUCKLE STREET 555-1234
YOURTOWN, USA 12345

Pay to the
Order of

BIG BANK
BIG BANK CORPORATION
BIGTOWN, U.S.A. 12345

FOR

⑈000056789⑈ 1234567B⑈

20

$

DOLLARS

SIGN HERE

00-000/000

CHARG·O·RAMA
GOLD

Member
Since 2003

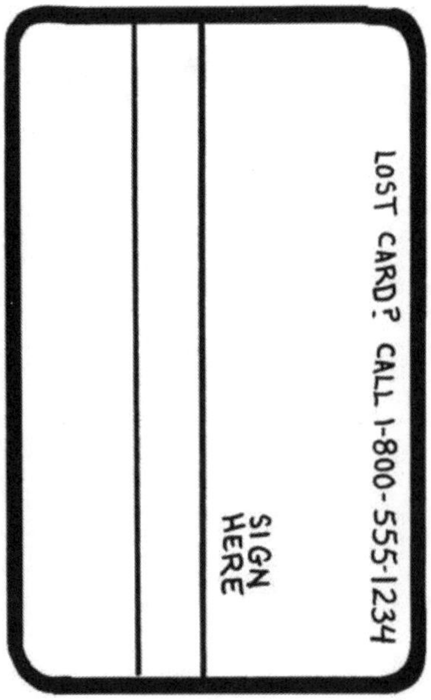

LOST CARD? CALL 1-800-555-1234

SIGN
HERE

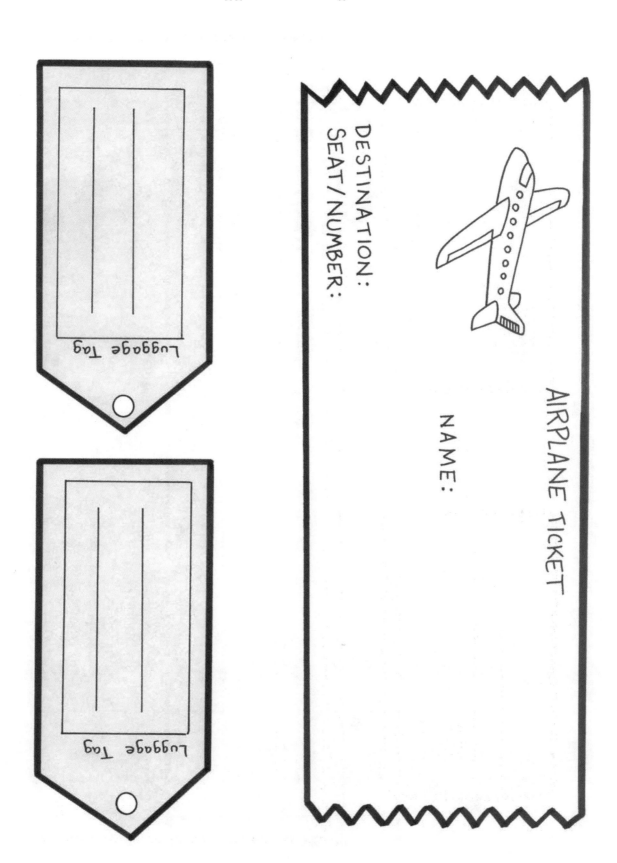

Luggage Tag

Luggage Tag

AIRPLANE TICKET

DESTINATION:

SEAT/NUMBER:

NAME:

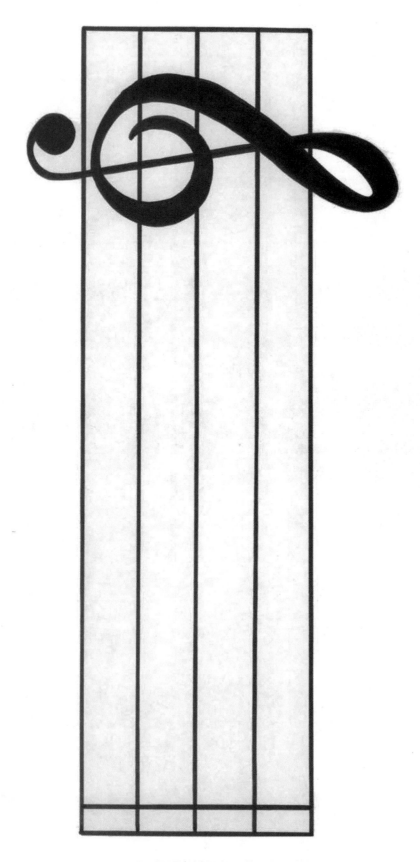

Dance Class Registration Form

Name of Dancer _____   Address: _____

Telephone Number _____   _____

Kind of Dance: _____   _____

Time: _____   Date: _____

Membership Card

_____ is a

Member of _____

Since (date) _____

Name of Book

Author

Date Completed

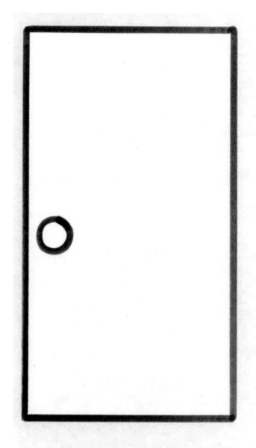

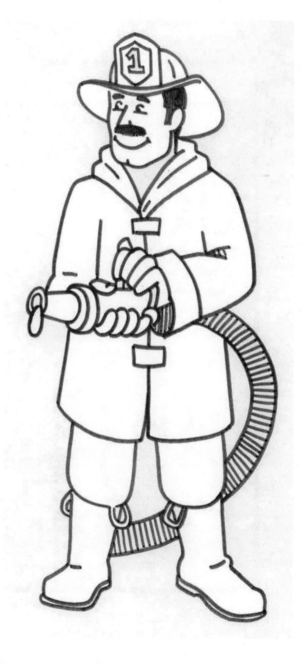

By:

Fire! Fire!

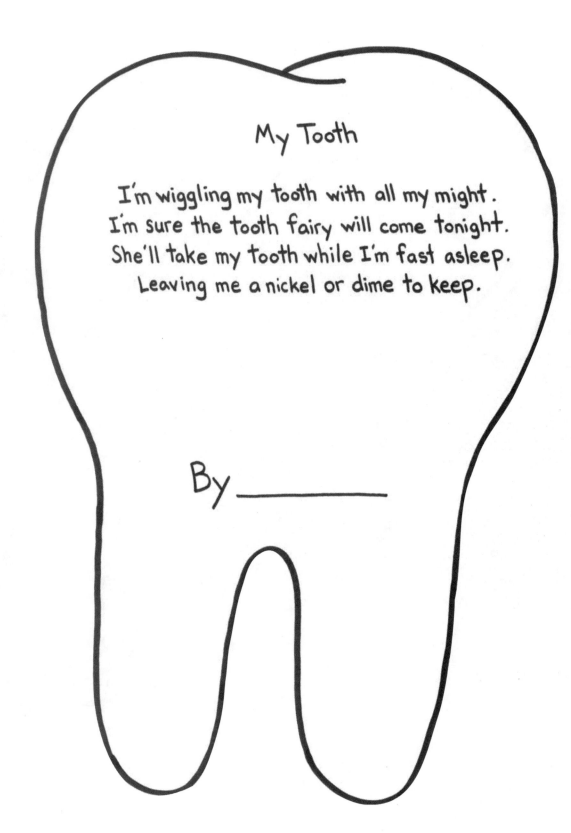

My Tooth

I'm wiggling my tooth with all my might.
I'm sure the tooth fairy will come tonight.
She'll take my tooth while I'm fast asleep.
Leaving me a nickel or dime to keep.

By _____

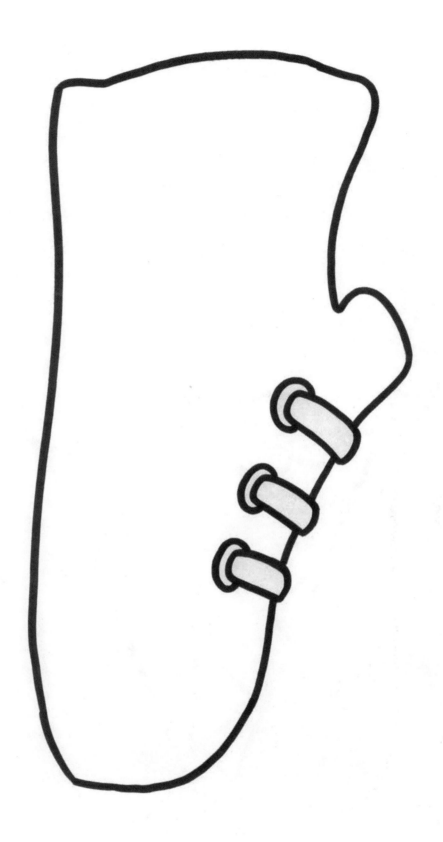

Yippety, splickety, lick ice-cream, there is a flavor that makes me scream.

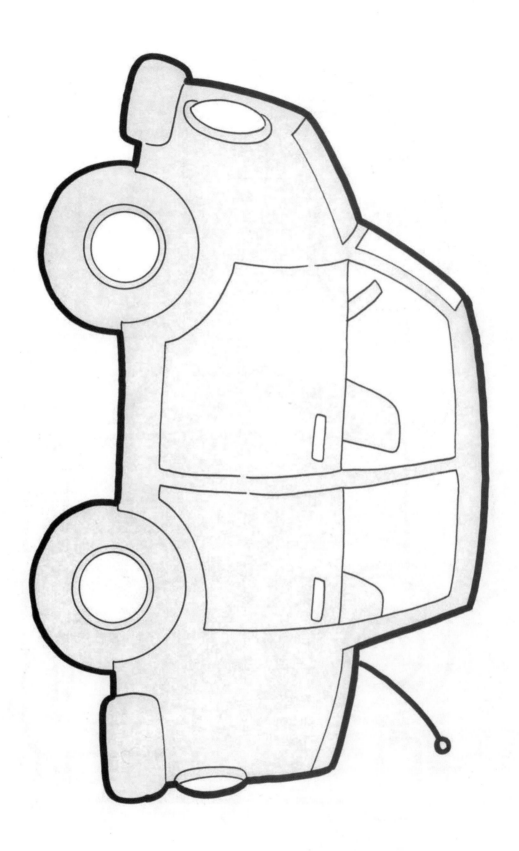

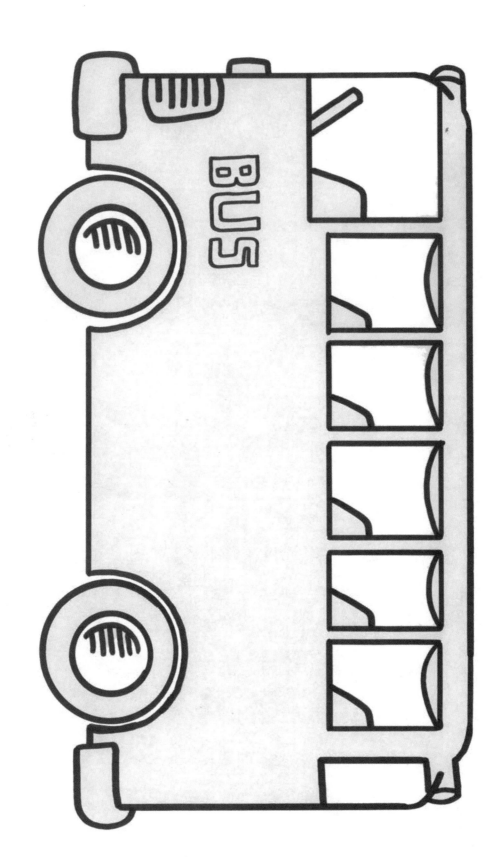

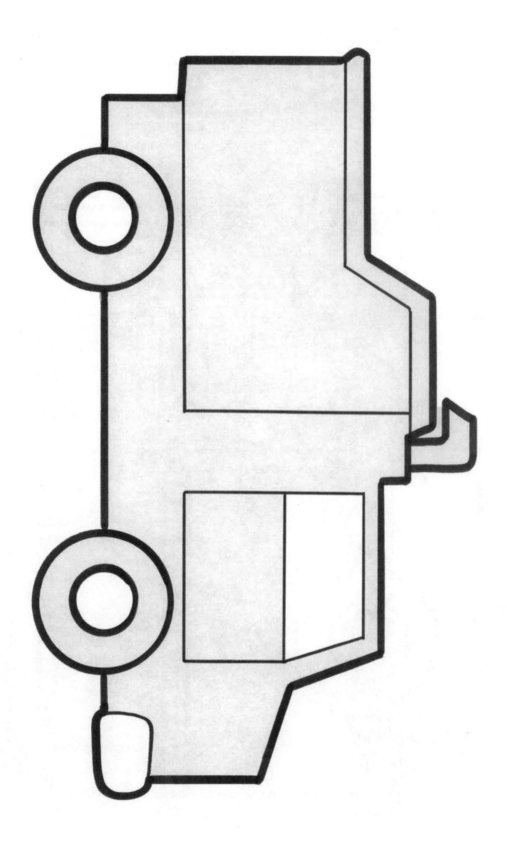

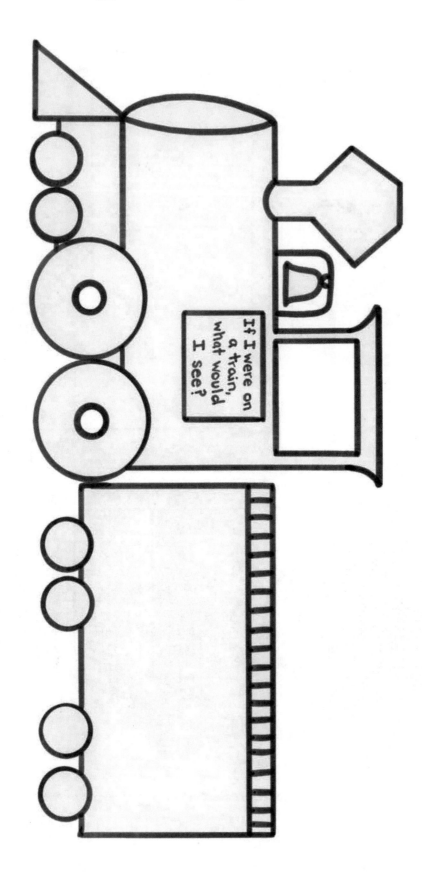

If I were on
a train,
what would
I see?

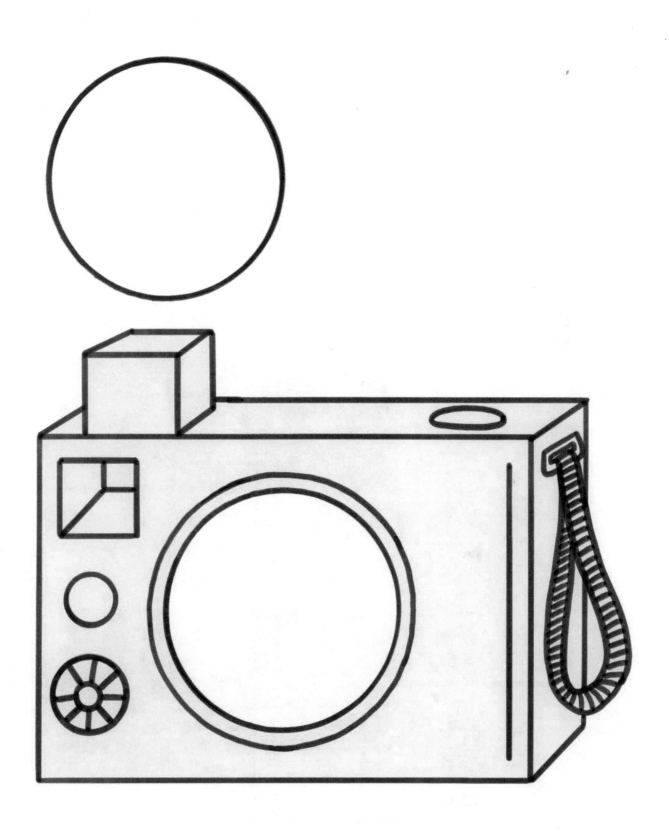

ABC's
For The
Piano

Written
And
Illustrated
By:

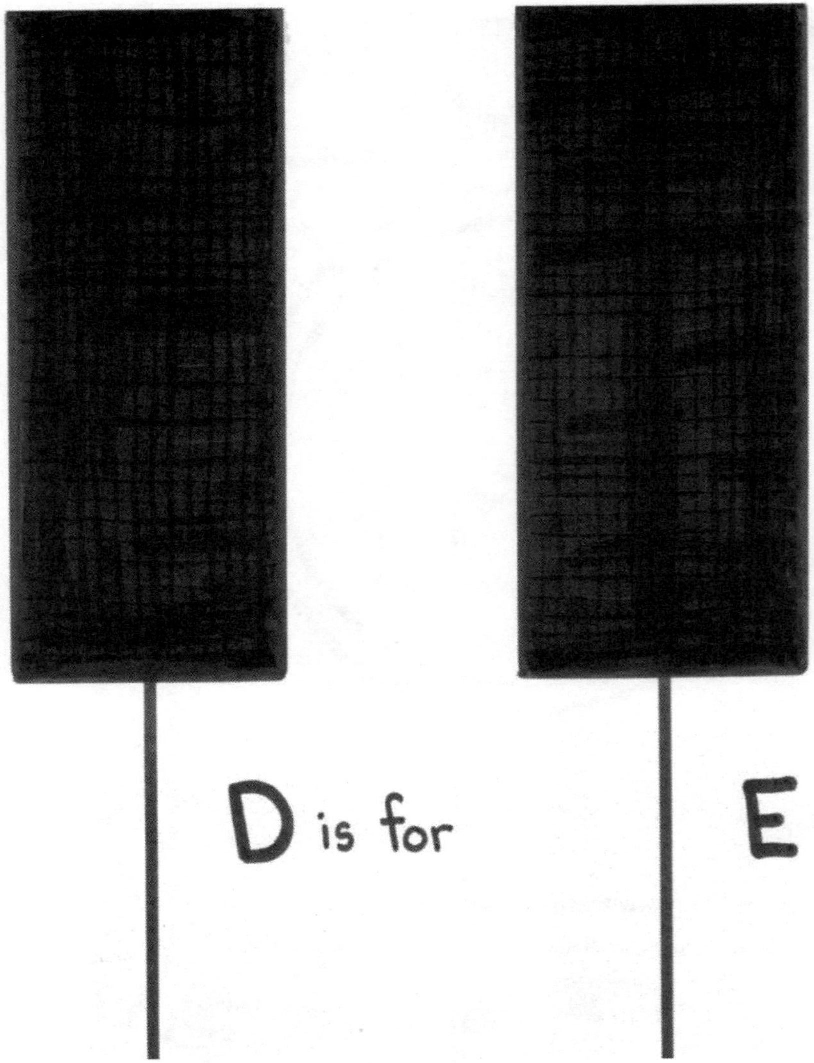

C is for

D is for

E is for

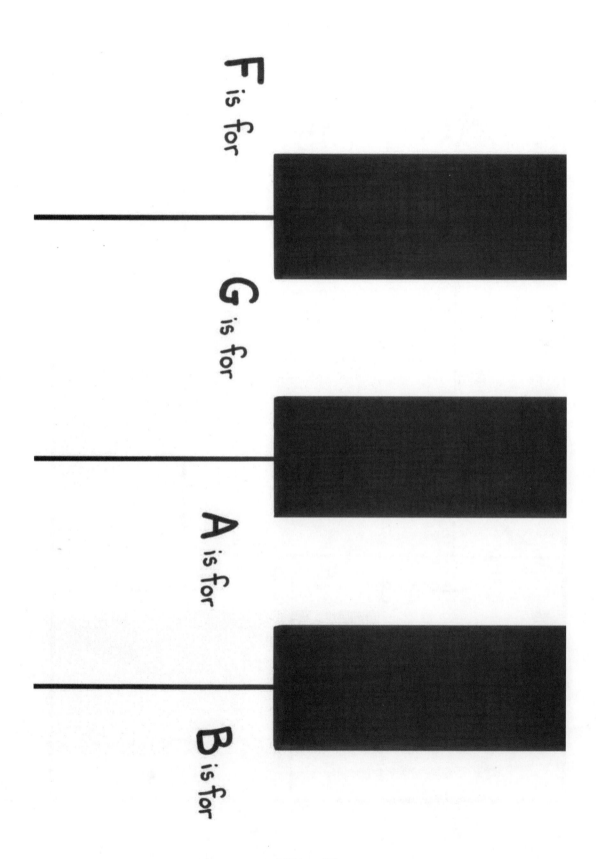

F is for

G is for

A is for

B is for

Our Class Newspaper

Favorite Books

Weather

People

Our World

Learning

Sports

© Gryphon House, Inc. • 800.638.0928 • www.gryphonhouse.com

Index

Children's Book Index

General Index

Children's Book Index

. . . . Index . . . .

Index

General Index